WIRING AN
AMERICAN DREAM

THE STORY OF BUDDY EIDEL
AND TRI-CITY ELECTRICAL CONTRACTORS INC.

BUDDY EIDEL
WITH KENNETH R. OVERMAN

Buddy Eidel

Written and Produced by   

www.BiographyMasters.com   kenoverman1@gmail.com

For my wife, Paula, who has always been by my side.
And for my parents, Charles and Elizabeth Eidel,
who supported me from the very beginning.

CONTENTS

I
FROM THE GARAGE UP

II
TOWARD HIGHER GROUND

III
PERSPECTIVES

IV
THE YEARS SINCE RETIREMENT

I
FROM THE GARAGE UP

1

Thanksgiving Day, 1971

A light north wind blew across the charred ruins. From where I stood, it smelled like a campfire recently doused with water. Some areas still smoldered beneath the ashes, and the acrid scent of burnt PVC from electrical wiring and supplies nearly made me sick: not so much from the smell, but the thought of that entire inventory going up in smoke. As my dad and I walked along the littered entrance of what used to be our office and warehouse, my foot crunched on a piece of our stationery. Only the top portion remained. "Tri-City Electrical Contractors, Inc."

Although the fire trucks left the night before, puddles of dark sooty water from their hoses remained here and there. A few metal chairs and file cabinets poked above the mountain of incinerated rafters, wallboard, roof tiles, and furniture. All that remained of the original structure was blackened perimeter walls surrounding an ugly 3,500-square-foot charred landfill. We walked in silence, weeping in disbelief. The only thing I knew was this was no accident.

***

Twenty-four hours earlier on the eve of Thanksgiving, my wife, parents, our three children and I sat around the living room of our Ski Mountain chalet outside Gatlinburg, Tennessee. We chatted about the

Aftermath of the fire

Remnants of the fire

Looking through accounts receivables

big news of the day: a hijacker named Dan Cooper parachuted from a Northwest Airlines 727 over Washington State with $200,000 in ransom. As our big oak wood fire beneath the hearth blazed away, we speculated on how long it would be until they apprehended Cooper, and if he had a chance to spend any of that money. A few hours later, I got the phone call with the news about the fire.

Dad and I spent the rest of the day alternating between shock, disbelief, and making calls. We had to get back to Florida as soon as possible, so we decided dad and I would catch the earliest flight out and have the rest of the family drive back later. The following morning, we landed in Orlando, picked up a rental car, and drove to the site of what used to be our company. Once the weeping subsided and some of the shock wore off, I knew what we had to do. It was already Friday, and we had three days to get the business up and going again.

We called all our office and field employees with the news, and soon our purchasing agent and two project managers showed up to help. The next day, Saturday, we drove one of our trucks to the George Stuart Office Supply store in downtown Orlando and hit the aisles. Dad, two office workers, and I pushed shopping carts up and down the corridors looking for essentials we'd need to operate the business on Monday morning. Yellow pads, pens, pencils, rulers, paper clips, an adding machine, a typewriter, and carbon paper, filled the baskets. After we checked out, we contacted my good friend, J.D. "Spider" Web, our Hughes Supply salesman. He took an order for a Monday morning delivery — enough to keep us going for the short run. Although they were closed on Saturdays, he took the order anyway. Indeed, J.D. Web came to our rescue.

By 1971, Tri-City had grown to the point where working out of our home was no longer an option. A good friend of mine named Hal Powers, who worked for Gale Realty in Maitland, was a commercial real estate agent. Hal had recently listed a combination office and warehouse on Atlantic Drive in Maitland. The man who owned it was a general contractor, so he'd left a few desks and other office furniture behind. It was sparse, but enough to get us by. Hal said we could use the space until

Atlantic Drive Office & Warehouse in Maitland, FL
Approximately 1972

we got back on our feet, and by early Monday morning we had moved everything in. Although crippled, we were as ready as we could be to get back to work. In fact, we had hardly missed a beat between closing on Wednesday the previous week and opening Monday morning.

The *Orlando Sentinel* and local TV stations spread the news as soon as the fire happened, so the entire city probably thought we were out of the game. With that in mind, as soon as our phones were hooked up, I called our general contractors to inform them we were still in business. I told them we had the full support of the community, including our suppliers and other creditors. One by one, they said they'd work with us. By late Monday night, we all heaved a collective sigh of relief. We were back in business and I felt a renewed determination to push ahead with a vengeance.

2

Not an Accident

In the days before computers and cloud backup services, important data like accounts receivable and payable were kept in file cabinets in the office's back closet. On certain occasions, older files were sent to an off-site location for safekeeping, or to please the IRS. So, nearly all of Tri-City's records were in the building when it burned. As soon as we got the wheels turning again, we went back to the site to salvage what we could. That's when we had a real stroke of good luck.

When the fire burned through the building's flat roof, the rafters supporting the roof and air conditioning system gave way and the whole thing fell down on top of the desk and file cabinet with our records. It collapsed with such force that the cooling tubes and reservoirs broke, pouring water over everything. The files were soaked, so nearly all of them made it through the fire intact.

Finding those documents was like discovering gold: now we'd know who owed what to whom and when it was due. We gathered the sopping wet records in boxes and took them over to dad's house, where he and mom carefully sorted through each one. Separating the pages, they spread them out on their driveway to let the Florida sun dry them out.

Although we couldn't account for everything, we salvaged enough to keep us going. Over the next few months, we collected payments from most of our clients and worked with our suppliers until everybody we owed was paid off. Just how much money we may have lost will never be known, but we still managed to salvage the majority of our receivables.

It would be quite some time, however, until we learned who torched our business.

***

The seventies marked a period of upheaval and change for union and nonunion shops across North America. Unions like the International Brotherhood of Electrical Workers (IBEW), with three-quarter of a million members today, have long been part of our nation's history. They fought for better pay, safer working conditions, health care, and retirement. Eventually, however, competitive nonunion shops infringed on what used to be exclusive union territory. So, it was only natural that aggressive, less-costly providers threatened a union system that had been in place for nearly a century and took more and more of the jobs.

As a result, a few union members took it upon themselves to disrupt advancing companies like ours. While I don't recall any specific threats, there was always the possibility that we could be challenged by some of the local guys. That might have been the case when we landed a job with the Brunswick Corporation's defense division in Deland, Florida. We were making inroads into some of the work the unions had, or thought they should have had.

From the day I started the business, I never signed a union agreement. That was true regardless of any job we may or may not have been awarded because of our status. I wasn't the only one who stuck to that policy: there were many other contractors who took the same position.

Several years later, after a similar fire destroyed a friend's fleet of service trucks, investigators caught the guy who burned down our building. He was a member of the United Association of Plumbers & Pipefitters (UAP&P). Now, we weren't in the plumbing business or anywhere near it, but the guy acted like he was a soldier in a union vs. nonunion war. He broke into our building with a five-gallon container of kerosene, dumped it on all the right places, and struck a match.

He wasn't captured until after he torched the headquarters of Airflow Designs, a heating and air conditioning business in Casselberry that belonged to a friend of mine, Roland "Cuz" Cousineau. At the end of the workday, Roland parked all his service trucks — about fifty of them — in his company yard. Long after dark, the man set the entire fleet on fire. By the time the fire trucks arrived, much of the fleet had been destroyed. That Mafia-style act landed the man in jail, and they ultimately linked him to the destruction of Tri-City's building.

Actions like these were meant to deter me from growing my company. In fact, the opposite happened: that fire made me more determined than ever to expand Tri-City as far and wide as I could.

But the will to keep going didn't come from me alone; I was helped by generations of tough Eidels who were born and bred in Germany.

A Friend in Need

The day before Thanksgiving in 1971, my family and I were out for dinner and Buddy was up in their mountain cabin with his family. We all worked out of our homes during the holidays, so after dinner I thought I'd drop by the office to pick up some plans. But when I came around the corner, I saw the entire building engulfed in flames! Buddy had built that business from the ground up, so when I saw that in front of me, I thought all of us were done.

That wasn't the case, because Buddy and his dad got right back and found a place where we could set up a temporary office. We gathered many of the records that somehow survived the fire, and spread them across the driveway of his dad's home to let them dry. Here's what was amazing: Although we couldn't find all our accounts receivable, many of our customers came forward to pay their obligations anyway. After the fire, Howard Palmer of Palmer Electric stopped by and offered any assistance he could at the time. That was significant since he was one of our major competitors.

David Beasley
Former Vice President, Tri-City
Electrical Contractors

3

It Started in Markelsheim

My dad, Charles Joseph Eidel, was born on August 2, 1909 in a little town named Markelsheim, in the southern part of Germany. That was nearly 110 years ago, a very long time ago now that I think of it. The Markelsheim township is much the same today as it was then: small, idyllic, and nestled in the rolling hills between Frankfurt and Nuremberg. The farming and wine making community looks much the same today as most German towns did back then: steep slate roofs, a tall Lutheran or Catholic steeple, a cozy town square, and small shops beneath rustic, gilded signs along narrow streets.

My father's father owned a butcher shop, a winery, and a restaurant. He also rented out a few of the rooms above the shop. Later, dad's brother

— we called him "uncle Alois"— took over the winery and the room rental business. Not long after, his son, Karl, and daughter-in-law, Edith, took over the butcher shop.

Elizabeth Augusta Vorpahl, my mother, entered the world on September 24, 1912, in Karlsruhe, about town about 100 miles west of Markelsheim. Karlsruhe lies on the west side of the Rhine River near France, close enough that she could walk to the French border and back in a day. Both her family and my father's endured World War I, which had a lot to do with their decision to emigrate.

About thirty years ago, my wife, Paula, and I flew to Germany and visited Markelsheim, and the home where dad was born. It was fun to see the railroad station on the edge of town, and my cousin Karl behind the counter of the family butcher shop. After seeing that beautiful little village, I wondered why dad had left it all to find a better life in America. Then I realized the physical and economic ravages of World War I must have been devastating, so unlike the tourist destination it was when I visited.

As for uncle Alois: he worked the vineyard for many years until he was no longer able.

***

During the century before my mother and her family arrived in New York, European and American steamship lines had developed business models around the steady flow of immigrants to America. As competition for passengers increased, so did the regulations, particularly in the area of health. Eventually, the steamship lines were responsible for medical examinations before passengers were allowed on board. Since most exams were done by doctors employed by the steamship lines, they sometimes overlooked everything but the most obvious defects.

My mother, her father, and her brother, Carl, arrived at Ellis Island in 1926. But during processing, officials rejected her father because of a head wound: something the examiner missed in his haste to depart

Bremerhaven. Apparently, her father had a large indentation in his skull from a World War I bullet wound, which was enough to catch the attention of the officials. I can't imagine the disappointment they felt after all that time and expense, only to see him sent back to Germany. Nevertheless, mom and her brother gave tearful goodbyes and continued on.

Since mom was ten years older than her brother, she was allowed to be his sponsor. There was a happy ending though: a few years later both of her parents were granted entry into the U.S., despite his head wound. They all settled in New York.

As dad related it to me, his brother, Alois, was so disappointed when dad left for America that he told him not to convince any of the other family members to go along. But dad managed to convince his sister, Frieda, and the two of them arrived at Ellis Island in 1928, two years after my mom. They both had relatives who sponsored them to come to this country, and eventually they both got their U.S. citizenship. Although they still hadn't met, they settled in Long Island and began to build a better life.

Dad was only nineteen when he arrived, but he was ambitious and highly motivated. It wasn't long until he landed a job as a mechanic with New York City's North Shore Bus Company. Later on, he worked for the city's Transit Authority repairing coin boxes on the turnstiles of the subways. Apparently, some passengers dropped slugs or other junk in the boxes to wrangle a free ride, but it usually jammed up the system. It was dad's job to keep them in working order.

Several years later, Elizabeth Vorpahl met Charles Eidel at a dance at one of the German-American clubs in New York. By then the two of them had achieved a fair command of English, so they had fun communicating in both languages. The following year, in 1934 — six years after dad arrived in the U.S. — they married in Astoria, Long Island. A year after that, Charles and Elizabeth Eidel took a steamer to Germany where they held another wedding ceremony for the benefit of family and friends. They returned to New York in time for my older brother, Charles Valentine, to be born on May 20, 1937, in Astoria. Twenty-two

Merkelsheim

Merkelsheim - The Eidel Homestead

months later, on March 12, 1939, in the same town, I entered the world as Helmuth Leo Eidel.

Several years ago, Paula and I went to the Family History Library in Salt Lake City, the genealogical arm of the Mormon Church, to study our family's immigration records. We were fascinated by how often our ancestors travelled back and forth between Germany and America because it had to have been very expensive. They made not one, but several trips between Bremerhaven and New York and we wondered where they got all the money for fares. In the 1930s the cost of a passage between Germany and the U.S. was around $188, the equivalent of $3,082 today. The cost of passage could be less expensive on certain ships that finagled profits by cramming 1,500 to 2,000 immigrants into extremely cramped quarters in the steerage area, or bowels of the vessel.

We concluded my ancestors made all those passages with help from family members, friends, or sometimes an American charitable organization. Usually only one or two members of a family went first, and when they earned enough money, they arranged for the rest of their family to follow.

4

Immigrant Life

My brother and I had a modest upbringing in New York, but for me it was a very happy one. We lived in an ordinary house at 82-19 Sixtieth Avenue, in Elmhurst, about four miles from the East River at Manhattan Island. My earliest recollection of our home was a brownstone, three-story attached townhouse. It had a garage in the basement along with a large adjoining game room, laundry room, and a steam heat boiler for the long, frozen winters.

In the summertime when it got really hot, mom and dad would treat my brother and I to a weekend trip to the Long Island shore. We swam at Rockaway Beach, or in a swimming pool in Valley Stream Long Island. We treasured those memorable trips in the family car, an old 1939 dark-blue Ford sedan. Between Christmas and summer breaks, my brother and I went to a New York public school (specifically PS #102), not far from our house. And, to continue the tradition of my father's roots in the old country, we attended Ascension Catholic Church on Queens Boulevard in Queens.

Mom had an old Maytag washer with one of those exposed, double-roll wringers on the top. One time my brother and I played around without paying attention and I got my hand caught in the wringer. The thing pulled my entire arm clear up to my shoulder before it let go. I wound up with a bad bruise and a lesson learned.

The driveway to the garage led down a steep grade, and on one snowy night, my mother tried to drive the car down to the garage without knowing how icy it was. The car slid down the driveway, right through the closed garage door.

Our living room, dining room, and kitchen were on the second floor, and on the third were three bedrooms. My brother and I shared a bedroom. Mom and dad had the second one, and uncle Carl — mom's brother who lived with us for a while — took the third. It was uncle Carl who used to tie our pajama feet together and roll us down the stairs. After Carl left, Mom used the room as a workplace for her spare job assembling greeting cards.

Since we were German, and because it was a necessity, both of them held full time jobs. Dad continued his work at the New York subway system and mother sewed in a factory on Long Island. She often brought work home and sewed after we were all in bed. She also earned money from the greeting card company. My brother and I spent many evenings after dinner and homework helping her fold, paste, and assemble cards. Dad also repaired National Cash Registers in the basement of our home. I remember him having register parts around the house soaking in cleaning fluid.

So, mom and dad were both very industrious. Dad could repair just about anything, and mom worked extra hard at various jobs. She'd learned how to paint houses from her father in Germany, and I remember her painting several rooms in our house. First, she would paint the walls with

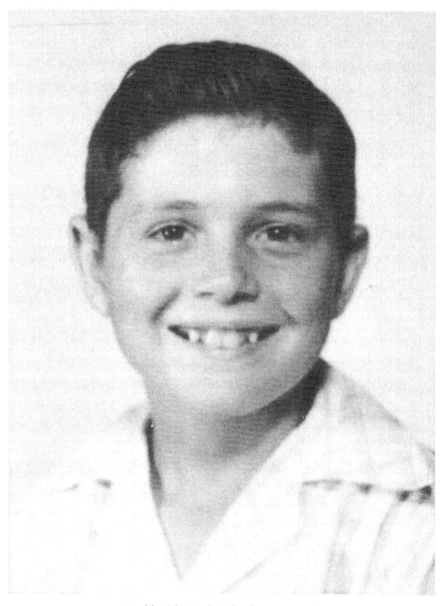

Buddy 4th Grade School picture 1948

a base coat and let it dry. Then, wearing rubber gloves, she'd take a rag soaked in paint of a darker or lighter shade and roll the rag over the wall. The result was an odd, uneven design that came out looking pretty good.

One of my first jobs in Queens was to shovel snow at a diner on Elliott Avenue; when I was done they gave me a hamburger for lunch. I also had a red Radio Flyer wagon I used for deliveries at the Bohack Grocery store on Elliott Avenue. They paid me all of a quarter, or sometimes fifty cents, to deliver groceries to elderly people a few blocks from the store.

During the war, my mom would prepare "care packages" for the relatives in Germany. She would send clothing and food items such as coffee, tea, sugar, powdered milk, and other essentials they could not get in Germany.

We called my grandfather, my mom's dad, "Opa", which means grandfather in German. Every Christmas for several years, Opa and "Oma" (German for grandmother) spent Christmas Eve with us. Well, Opa would dress up in a big ol' Santa Clause suit and surprise us with presents before we went to bed. We'd be sitting around the tree and suddenly Opa would say he had to go out to get a pack of cigarettes. Then while he was gone, Santa Claus knocked on our door carrying a big sack on his back. With a "Ho, ho, ho!" he'd go around the room passing out presents. One of the last childhood Christmases I remember, he had rigged his sack so when he entered the house the bottom opened, spilling all the presents onto the floor. He had apparently gotten tired of passing out the presents one by one.

It took a while for my brother and me to figure out the real story, but until then it was a lot of fun. Opa passed away the year before we moved to Florida, but Oma stayed with us for a while after that.

5

Toward Warmer Climes

While dad was born Catholic, mom was Lutheran. In Germany, the two religions claim about half of Germany's 65 percent Christian

Buddy and Brother Chuck in Elmhurst

population. Most of Markelsheim's residents were active Catholics, and dad's sister, who traveled with him to the U.S., also practiced Catholicism. I suppose that's the reason Charles and I were raised Catholic. To this day, all of our New York cousins are very devout Catholics.

Religion aside, I'm very thankful I was raised in an environment with a solid work ethic. Both parents were very strict, so the house rules for my brother and me were simple: work hard and stay out of trouble. To that end, we always had chores to do at home. What helped to balance it all was mother's German cooking. She was excellent!

I have fond memories of uncle Carl. He lived with us for a while in Elmhurst before he married and started a family in Astoria, Long Island. He was a fun, interesting guy who was often up to something or joking around. Carl was also a very smart man who was always inventing some kind of gadget. One of the projects he developed was a small, car wheel-balancing machine. It worked, and he traveled across the country to sell his invention. Later, in 1970, he caught the Eidel vision and he and his family moved to Longwood, Florida. He opened a Mr. Muffler shop in nearby Sanford with his son Carl Jr. It's still operating as of this writing.

After Carl semi-retired from the Muffler Shop in 1997, I tapped his creative juices to improve a "chop saw" we used in our business to cut metal-clad cable. The saw was designed to cut the metal jacket without cutting the wires inside, and we used it in our prefab operation. The original saw did the job, but it wasn't very efficient. So, uncle Carl worked on the device and improved it tremendously. Then, like his wheel-balancer, he manufactured the saw and sold it nationwide. I'd like to note that the original saw was developed by Don White of Riviera Electric in Denver, Colorado, one of our Quality Circle members I'll tell you about later in the book. But uncle Carl's improvement really set it apart from the original.

***

Buddy in 6th grade at Lyman School – apx 1951

Meanwhile, back in New York, Dad's health eventually took a turn for the worse. He was diagnosed with rheumatic heart disease, and his doctor told him he needed to get out of the cold subways and extreme climate. The message was clear: stay in New York and shorten his life, or move to warmer climes. So, mom and dad left us in the city while they headed south to explore the bottom of the country. A nice, older woman, Ann Cihal, who dad befriended at his subway job, babysat my brother and me while our parents were in Florida looking for a new home. Later, the Cihal's would follow us to Florida to settle in Union Park in East Orlando.

So, we left New York and settled in Central Florida. That was in 1948, and just in time for the most intense hurricane to make landfall in the state since 1935. In the days before hurricanes had proper names, they called it the "Labor Day Hurricane." The move was a big leap of faith for my parents because neither of them had transferrable skills for the Land of Sunshine. Soon after we arrived, they decided the best way to earn a living was to run a motel. And that's what they did.

Dad bought a few acres of land outside Fern Park and built seven small cottages to rent out. They christened it the "Bluebird Motel," a name mom came up with, although she couldn't explain the significance. She just liked the name.

6

Sinking Roots

Everybody in the family worked to help our common cause. Mom took care of the rental cottages and worked as an assistant chef at a famous 1950s restaurant in Fern Park, Freddie's Steak House. Many prominent people around Orlando went there because it was reputed to have the best steaks in town. Sometimes, when I finished my after-school job, I'd walk down to Freddie's and mom would cook me the best steak in a big black iron skillet. I'd sit on an orange crate outside the back door of the kitchen and devour it. To me, it really was the best steak in town. After that, I was good to go for the rest of the evening.

Mom also worked part-time at a sewing factory in nearby Sanford. My brother, Charles, worked at the Prairie Lake Drive-In Theatre's concession stand. And, like many of our friends, he also worked at the Sanford Orlando Kennel Club, cooling down the greyhounds after the races.

I did my part by cutting grass and running a paper route. At fourteen, I got my first set of wheels, a Harley-Davidson Model 165, a small two-stroke motorcycle. Then, I graduated to a much larger Triumph motorcycle. Because I didn't have enough body weight to pump the kickstarter, I had to run alongside the bike, quickly jump on and pop the clutch to start it.

Later on, I pumped gas after school at Sweeney's Shell gas station in Fern Park, when gas cost twenty-five cents per gallon and "self-serve" pumps were unheard of. The owner, John Sweeney, had two children who had to work just like we did. Together, we swept the entire driveway of the station, including the 200-foot frontage road. I thought it was a huge job, but Mr. Sweeney made an early impression on me about having an excellent, hard work ethic.

A year later, Mr. Sweeney sold the gas station to Larry DePerch, and I continued to work for him. Mr. DePerch taught me a lot about repairing cars and inspired me to take a few high school credits at an Orlando automotive vocational school. When I was finished, I knew how to tear down and clean a two-barrel carburetor and replace a set of points in a distributor.

My brother and I attended the old Lyman School, which contained all twelve grades in one building. It wasn't all work though: we were also active in sports. My bother played American Legion Baseball, and I played Little League Baseball in a vacant lot where Winter Park Memorial Hospital is today. We both caddied for golfers at the downtown Winter Park Golf Course. Later, I joined the baseball team at the Boys Club league in Orlando, a spot currently occupied by the Amway Center sports arena.

In 1951, I helped my dad's friend, Walter Allender, plant an orange grove. Walt and his wife were guests at my parents' motel. While there, Walt purchased a large piece of acreage on U.S. 17, across from what is now Seminole State College of Florida. Walt built a house there, then planted forty acres of orange groves on the rest of the property. On weekends, dad and I helped him with the planting. Many years later, after Walt and his wife sold the property, the orange groves – like so many others in the area – became the target of development. No longer adorned by oranges, Walt's property became "Flea World," one of the largest flea markets in the country. Today, Flea World is closed and the property is up for redevelopment.

***

Unfortunately, my parent's motel never became self-sustaining, so Dad started to look for a full-time job to make ends meet. At first, he tried a few odd jobs but his credentials as a New York subway coin machine repairman didn't go far in Florida. There were bus companies in Orlando's public transportation system, but they didn't use coin boxes.

Eventually, he landed a job with the Dr. Phillips Company in Orlando as a mechanic's helper on their machinery. The company owned large tracts of orange groves and ran an orange packing and processing facility in Fairvilla, north of Orlando. Dad, who was in his late thirties, became friends with a supervisor, Willie Barnes, Sr. Willie took dad under his wing and taught him how to weld and do other jobs.

Many years later, Willie's kindness paid itself forward. Dad never forgot his kindness and years later, when our business was doing well, dad got a call from Willie. Apparently, his son, Willie Jr., had gotten into trouble and needed a job. He asked dad if we could help, and dad was happy for a chance to return the favor. We hired Willie Jr. as an electrical helper in the company, and that was all he needed to move in the right direction.

A few years after the Dr. Phillips Company hired dad, good fortune showed up in the form of a man who rented one of our cottages. The renter, Carl Barber, was working with Modern Electric Company in Jacksonville on a contract at the nearby Naval Air Station Sanford, installing underground lighting and approach lights for the airport runways. Carl and dad got to talking and soon became friends. Later, Carl helped dad get a job with the local union contracted to install the runway lights. Dad had just turned forty, but the union accepted him into the training program anyway. That's how my father became a card-carrying apprentice and union member electrician working on an airfield lighting system.

I was a teenager when that happened. And while it may have appeared that I ignored everything around me, as teenagers often do, I was actually paying close attention. It could have been my German upbringing, but when it came to the way my parents put bread on the table, I really took it to heart. I scrutinized what my father did for a living, and realized the kind of sacrifices he made to get there.

After dad got comfortable with his position, he started taking on small electrical repair jobs on the side, mostly for his friends. I watched that, too, and that's how I became interested in the electrical trade.

7

A Used Truck and a Vision

The older I grew, the more I wanted to earn my own way in life. I started banging around two or three jobs, and one of them was with the A. DUDA & Sons Company in Oviedo, near Orlando. DUDA was, and still is, a large Slovakian-owned produce and real estate company not far from where we lived. I was one of their couriers who drove a delivery truck for their supply houses in Oviedo. Later on, I worked at an auto body shop where I sanded cars and learned a bit about bodywork. That didn't last long though. Throughout all my jobs and experiments, I never lost interest in what my father did for a living. The electrical trade still fascinated me.

Dad helped me get a job as an apprentice electrician at the Glenn L. Martin Company, about four miles south of Orlando. I worked full-time in the field doing electrical work, but I mostly dug ditches and attended a union-sponsored apprenticeship school in the evenings. I knew I wanted to stay in the electrical trade, and if digging ditches would help me get there, youth and enthusiasm propelled me to do the best I could. Unfortunately, I had a couple of bad experiences in my early union days, so I quit. I decided I would work as a nonunion member for the long run, or not at all.

My next job was in the parts department at the Joseph L. Rozier Machinery Company, where I had been introduced by Bob Hattaway's uncle, "Hat" Hattaway. They assigned me to the parts department where they trained me to sell parts for bulldozers and Caterpillar equipment. I did my best, but I was still hooked on the electrical trade and spent much of my time plotting how I could get back in the business. I was confident I'd learned enough in apprentice school to do a decent job, but I hated the idea of joining a union again, even if they would take me back.

***

Not long after I decided to re-enter the electrical field, a good friend, Talley Hattaway, Bob Hattaway's father, encouraged me to start my own business. I was friends with Bob's son, Bobby, and his daughter, Francis, and we often went to Talley's house in Orienta Gardens on Sundays to waterski on the lake in front of his house. Talley's wife, Alma, always fixed a big lunch for us. Later in 1957, I bought a home site from Talley where I built my first home. That's when he told me about all the construction and homebuilding going on in his area and encouraged me to get involved by starting my own business. He also recommended a few subcontractors and suppliers for me to contact.

That was all I needed to hear. I had read in the paper that Southern Bell Telephone was upgrading its fleet, so when the company put its used service trucks out to pasture, I bought an old green telephone truck at auction for $500. As a first time independent electrical contractor, it suited me just fine. The truck was five years old and, though a bit dog-eared, it came with shelves for tools and materials. That was a good start, but what happened next really put me on course to launch my own company.

In 1958, dad and I talked about his involvement in the business, and I really think I scared the hell out of him. After all, he was fairly successful and in good financial shape, so he didn't want to lose it on his nineteen-year-old son. But he went along with it anyway because he knew I was serious. Then he did an extraordinary thing: he mortgaged their house and used the money to help me get going.

With around $30,000 in capital, we got lines of credit with electrical wholesale outlets for materials and supplies. I say "we" because dad was all in right from the start. He also co-signed for a line of credit with Hughes Electrical Supply so I could buy even more material.

After the mortgage, dad kept working long enough to get my company going. At the time, he was still on board with Modern Electric projects at the Sanford Naval Air Station, about twelve miles from where we lived. Although I went independent nonunion, he stayed on with the electrical union's Local 606 because the cash flow was good. That's how — at the age of nineteen and with the incalculable value of dad's faith and monetary assistance — Tri-City Electrical Contractors was born.

Later, dad went to work on a joint venture project with Johnson Electric of Orlando and Fischbach & Moore of New York, constructing a new Glenn L. Martin plant on Sand Lake Road, in Orlando. When the project was complete, dad went back to the Modern Electric Company to work on an airfield lighting job in Paris Island, South Carolina. Now a commuter, he drove the 640-mile round trip, coming home on the weekends. Needless to say, it wasn't long before he got sick of spending so much time behind the wheel, and not being with his family.

FLORIDA INDUSTRIAL COMMISSION

DEPARTMENT OF APPRENTICESHIP

Date of Issue __Nov. 25, 1957__ No. **16293**

CERTIFYING THAT __HELMUTH L. EIDEL__

Indentured as an __Electrician__ Apprentice

in accordance with the terms and conditions of the Florida Apprenticeship law (Chapter 23934, Acts of 1947).

Orlando Electrical JAC

Date Apprenticeship Began __Nov. 12, 1957__

Term of Apprenticeship __48 Months__

Credit for Previous Experience __4 Months__

Director

Buddy's Electrical License

Our first service truck

Fortunately, Tri-City had grown to the point where he considered joining our company full-time. That's what he did in 1960, two years after our company was born.

Dad immediately fit right in. He paired up with an Irishman, Murray O'Flynn, and the two used an old, yellow milk truck as their Tri-City work vehicle. Murray was a large man with a red beard and red hair who chewed tobacco, and the two got along real well. In fact, watching the two of them, my short German father and the huge Irishman, was downright comical.

Easy Rider

I first met Buddy at Lyman High School back in the fifties: I graduated in 1955 and Buddy was about three years behind me. My graduating class had thirteen students, one girl and the rest boys. The girl was the homecoming queen, of course.

Buddy was very popular during school and very full of himself, as I'm sure he is today. I remember when he got into some kind of trouble with Mr. Douglas, our principal, who took exception to something Buddy did in class. In those days a principal could paddle students on the behind for misbehaving. Well, Buddy wasn't about to let that happen, so Mr. Douglas expelled him for three days. Buddy got so upset, he rode his motorcycle up the seven steps of the school entrance, into the hallway, and past the principals' office. Then he took a sharp left and went down another hallway before exiting the back door and down the stairs. Principal Douglas expelled him for another three days.

Buddy was a pretty good stock car driver, too. Several of us were in the game and raced around a dirt track in Deland. About seven of us had cars. We'd work on our cars throughout the week and race them on Sunday. Buddy had the best car, and the fastest, because he put more time into his car than anyone else.

I was still in school when Buddy started Tri-City in his home, which really makes him an example of the American Dream. He's done a lot of electrical work for us through the years, and I always go back to Tri-City because I know him personally and because he does such a great job. He is a shining example of what can be accomplished if you work hard and keep your nose to the grindstone. Seeing what he started in the carport of his house, and what it is today, shows he's a great example for his city and the state.

Bob Hattaway - Member of the Florida House of Representatives, 1974 - 1982

8

Thanks to Sputnik

Our first company office was located at my home. Although the house had all of 1,200 square feet of living space, the family room and spare bedroom became our office while a tiny utility room served as our warehouse. In early mornings, we staged the day's work in the garage.

Wiring the average home only took a few days. Since jobs like those were relatively easy to pick up, I tended to focus on the Orienta Gardens projects with the help of Talley Hattaway. If a job was profitable enough, I hired an extra electrician so we could get it done within a day or two. On the other hand, if I was between projects I worked as a carpenter's helper until I landed the next wiring job.

Those small, startup contracts became my bread and butter during the first years of my company. It seemed like more and more houses were under construction all over, and the reason stemmed from something that happened the previous year. The event was called Sputnik, and it placed Florida on the world map.

The Soviet Union, our country's formidable post-World War II enemy, launched the first man-made satellite into space in 1957. For weeks after the launch, Americans watched the 184-pound device do nothing more than beep and blink its way across the sky. We were infuriated. We thought we might have lost the Space Race. Politicians and the public demanded funding to beat the Russians. As a result, then-Senate Majority Leader Lyndon Johnson pushed the National Aeronautics and Space Act through Congress. On October 1, 1958, President Dwight D. Eisenhower established the National Aeronautics and Space Administration (NASA).

The government chose to build Cape Canaveral roughly forty miles from Altamonte Springs. Thousands of workers flooded America's new spaceport, transforming the area into a hub of aeronautics and manufacturing. Cities near the Cape, such as Titusville, Cocoa, Melbourne and Orlando, grew rapidly. Factories producing crucial products for the space program emerged across the state. Space exploration and related industries pumped billions of dollars in federal funds into Florida's economy. The Space Age changed our state forever, and so our company grew.

As the jobs kept coming, I aggressively pursued every opportunity. If I couldn't hire additional employees, I did it myself or asked dad to help me. When I had too much to do, I somehow found more workers.

One of them was Fred Kroker, who worked for us nearly forty years. I remember when Fred, with his jet-black hair and 5'6" frame, walked through the door of our living room in 1960. Fred came from a construction background, and his father was a block mason. Fred was a hard worker and of German descent, like me, so we immediately hit it off. At the time, he still worked for Star Electric, but I believe we offered more pay. I needed the extra help, so I didn't worry too much about the other company and hired him that morning.

Fred, whose real name is Manfred, started out in our residential single-family homes, often the high-end luxury homes. He ran the residential department until Rance Broderick took it over. As the company grew, Fred grew with it. In 1968, he came inside to become one of our first residential estimators.

Like me and several others, Fred took plans home on evenings and weekends. His wife, Judy, helped him with takeoff, the original estimate, and counting fixtures. Like me, Fred was very frugal and tried to save our company money when he could. He even scolded warehouse employees when they threw away scrap wire that Fred thought was useable.

Fred's career with Tri-City was typical of so many Tri-City employees who were getting started in the field. He worked his way up through the ranks, from helper to apprentice to journeymen, superintendent, and project manager, before moving into estimating and department management.

***

Meanwhile, dad helped out when he wasn't at his full-time job, and mom pitched in with the bookkeeping. As usual, she also kept us all well fed with her German cuisine.

In the initial stages of our business, I found myself eating from the "low hanging fruit" of subdivision homes. The jobs were plentiful, and there was something about working on homes in a concentrated area that spawned more business. Many new clients came to us through word of mouth, mostly those who spread our name to others looking for good providers. But there was something else about our company they liked: people wanted to work with a local organization. They tended to hire a company known by the locals, one that was accessible, and accountable. Sensing that, I realized we needed a name that would convey those values to the general public outside of housing tracts. I wanted to reassure current and potential clients that we were their local contractor. So, when they asked where we worked, I said we covered Altamonte Springs, Casselberry, and Fern Park, all within twenty square miles. Hence the "Tri-City" moniker. In the early days, towns were much smaller than they are today, so the name worked well for a while.

When our work and scope expanded, and I landed a contract in Longwood, I said, "Our three cities are Altamonte Springs, Casselberry, and Longwood." Wherever we worked, we covered one of the tri-cities. Later when the business really took off, my tri-cities became Tampa, Fort Myers, and Miami. I'm not sure if that kind of marketing would find its way into the MBA textbooks, but people felt like we were their hometown company, so it worked quite well.

Once we had a name, I started advertising. I made large cardboard signs and tacked them in obvious places where passers-by could read, "Electrical work by Tri-City Electric." That, along with word of mouth and networking with contractors, grew the business even more. As a result, we made more money. As it came in, I plowed it all back into the business.

9

A Benevolent Supplier

We had made it through our first year and a half in business. I can't say exactly how much we cleared, but it was far less than we had hoped because a contractor ran off with our money. Our financials as of December 31, 1961 showed a gross revenue of $127,136 and a net profit of $18,990. I guess that wasn't too bad for a startup company after all.

One of our early major contracts was in a development near Longwood, about four miles north of our office. It was the early sixties and we'd been in business about three years. I heard about the construction going on in that community, so I tracked down the main contractor and made an offer. Fortunately, I was the lowest bidder, so we got the contract. I already had four people working for Tri-City, so I was able to jump right on it. Four months later, that project nearly brought my business to a dismal end. Here's what happened.

We originally contracted to wire several houses in the community, and I estimated each unit would cost around $1,500 for wiring, supplies, and labor prior to drywall installation. Other electrical components would be installed after the drywall, but that was a separate part of the contract. According to the deal, we wouldn't get paid until the job was done, so I had to buy the materials on credit from Hughes Supply. Having that credit line enabled me to pay my workers every week until the job was over, at which time Tri-City would be paid.

The story I heard (after the fact) was the lead contractor who hired us took the prepayment money from his clients and bought virgin timberland in British Honduras. It was a "speculative investment strategy," and when it all went south, the contractor filed for bankruptcy and disappeared. Tri-City wasn't the only contractor left holding the bag: all the other subs were left hanging as well.

Until the Longwood project, we had only worked on one or two homes at a time. So, that multiple-unit project was a big deal for us. When it was all over, I lost about $14,000 in a three-month period, which was a lot of money in the sixties. I still had to pay my workers since none of it was their fault. The biggest problem, however, was my debt with Hughes Supply, which made up the majority of project expenses.

As I mentioned, Hughes Supply was our first major business partner. They were a large, highly respected company, and our first Hughes sales rep was a tall, intelligent guy named Dooley Shurbert. Dooley would call me the night before his scheduled visit to determine the needs of my project site, and the next day he would meet me to take my order. Over time, Dooley became a real friend and that was the reason we hit it off so well with Russell Hughes, the owner of the company. But now that I was cash-strapped, how in the world could I tell them I couldn't pay?

I distinctly remember the long drive across Orlando to Russell's office on Central Avenue. As I wove through traffic, I rehearsed the conversation over and over — how I'd tell him I couldn't pay for the material. It wouldn't make a bit of difference that we were beat out of it through no fault of mine. I imagined him looking at me with steely eyes and saying, "So what? That happens when you own your own business, so think of a way to pay me, or else."

Halfway up the stairs to his second-floor office, I saw an imposing picture of Russell in a place that was impossible to miss. He had the expression and look of a bulldog, and the caption read, "Give me my G.. D… Money!"

At the ripe age of twenty, I can't tell you how much that sign intimidated me. Then and there I decided to tell that man the absolute truth, expect the worst, and find a way to pay him back.

To my great relief, Russell wasn't at all like that bulldog portrait. I explained what happened in detail and he was perfectly fine with it as long as I stuck to my word about paying him back. I knew my redemption would come by doing just that. Relatively new to the construction industry, I didn't know it wasn't the first time Russell had dealt with late payments. That sort of thing happened all too frequently.

We worked out a payment plan, and in due time I paid back every cent I owed. Because of that, I continued to purchase most of our electrical materials from Hughes. If we ever ran short of cash and had a hard time paying our materials bill, Hughes always worked with us. It's worth noting that because of their consistency and excellent service, Hughes remained one of our closest partners.

Russell's nephew, David, eventually took over the company and grew it until they went public. Not long after, Home Depot purchased the company, so Hughes Supply no longer exists. Fortunately, David has

COMMERCIAL AND RESIDENTIAL ELECTRICAL CONTRACTORS

173 PLUMOSUS ST.   TRI-CITY ELECTRIC   ALTAMONTE SPRINGS, FLA.

P. O. Box 495

PHONES
MIDWAY 7-0649
MIDWAY 4-9821

Winter Park Federal & Loan Association:

Winter Park, Fla.

Att: Mr. Jackson.

Balance Sheet as of Dec. 31, 1961.

Assets:		Liabilities:	
Cash in Banks	417.51	Accounts Payable	6,073.49
Acct. Receivable	11,052.74	Notes Payable	8,919.45
Inventories	8,741.08	F.I.C.A. Tax withheld	333.13
Fixed Assets	6,206.32	Fed. Income Tax "	252.70
		Sales Taxes	44.82
Total Assets	26,417.65	Accrued Fla. Unemploymt	88.00
		Total Current Liab.	15,711.59
		Capital Stock	500.00
		Net Worth	10,206.06
		Total Liabilties	26,417.65

Statement From Jan. 1, 1961 To Dec. 31, 1961.

Net Sales	127,136.55
Cost of Sales	88,973.15
Gross Profit	38,163.40
Total Exp.	29,172.79
Net Profit	18,990.61

Signed : *Charles J. Eidel*

Our 1961 P & L statement

remained a good friend and we get together at the Interlachen Country Club now and then.

I never actually met the contractor who stiffed us. I only knew about them because their names were on one of their checks that we did receive.

Meet "The Bull"

I first got to know Buddy on a professional level through a business arrangement, when we supplied their electrical equipment. A little later we got to know each other more through golf, because my wife plays golf and so do Buddy and Paula. Those two make a great team on the course, and in their business as well.

I think there are similarities between Buddy's business and ours. When I first got out of law school in 1968, I went to work at the warehouse at my father's company. Later in the seventies, he turned the company over to me in the same way Buddy's father was also in the electrical business with him.

I remember the grand opening of their new warehouse and offices, when they invited suppliers and others in their sphere of business. I went with our salesmen, and Buddy showed us around the facility. When we walked by his dad's office, Mr. Eidel hollered at me to come in to talk. I did, and he went on to tell the story of when Tri-City first went into the business back in the fifties. Mr. Eidel told me he visited my uncle Russell to ask if they would give them credit to do business when Tri-City first opened their doors. Well, my uncle Russell was a tough old guy, which is why they called him "The Bull."

When Mr. Eidel first met The Bull, he said he was kind of scared, but my uncle said he would give them credit. When Mr. Eidel was about to leave, uncle Russell said, "Oh, and if you don't pay me, I'll have to whip your ass." That says something about how they did business in those days. Mr. Eidel always liked to tell that story.

Actually though, it's the nature of the supply end of the business that we sometimes don't get paid until the contractor is paid. And occasionally, contractors might get a customer that doesn't want to pay, so they had to be tough about it. But, I can tell you this: Tri-City was always one of those clients who always paid on time. Their word was their word, and if they had trouble, they were always able to work it out with us.

Buddy is an unusual person. He greets everyone with a smile, and when you talk with him he's a quality person who is always cordial. Still, he can be a tough businessman when he needs to. On the personal side, Buddy and Paula always seem to have fun together. On the business side, there's no question that Buddy Eidel impacted the electrical industry in Florida in a powerful way. He remains a highly respected businessman throughout our industry.

David Hughes, Hughes Supply

The Hughes situation wasn't the only thing that went wrong in our early years. A tenant who rented a bungalow from my parents, Clarence

Klint, was a retired carpenter from Flint, Michigan, who spent his winters in Florida with his wife and occasionally worked for my dad. One day when Clarence was helping demolish a building for my dad, a large section of wall toppled over and landed directly on him. He was instantly killed. That was tough for me and even harder on dad. But such things happen all too frequently in our line of work.

10

Aiming Higher

I had never intended to start a mom and pop business and leave it at that. Ever since the day I drove that used Bell Telephone truck off the lot, I knew I wanted a big company. The only way I could achieve that was to get better and better with our service and reach for larger contracts.

Like most contractors, we sought projects through any source we could. So, we took advantage of the Dodge Report and the CFBE, the Central Florida Builders Exchange, for a compilation of construction projects in the area, and submitted our contractor's request for bids through them. General contractors, builders in charge of the day-to-day oversight of construction, vendors, trades, solicit bids from subcontractors such as Tri-City and myriad others. Naturally, builders wanted to shop around for the best subcontractor possible, so they deposited their plans in the exchange where all the licensed subs could take a crack at it. The CFBE printed a weekly bulletin for projects in the Orange, Seminole, Volusia, and Osceola counties. The Dodge folks mailed three-by-five cards to us almost every day with addresses, project size, names of general contractors, and a thumbnail rundown of the project.

If we were interested, we went down to the CFBE "plan room" where broad tables were available to roll out the large project blueprints. We would pull up our sleeves and work out the takeoff right then and there, or we could check the plans out overnight and do the numbers in our office. For an initial takeoff, we transferred the linear feet of conduit, wire, outlets, receptacles, switches, air conditioning units, and all related electrical items required for the project based on the main contractor's blueprints. Later on, we'd work out the project time and cost in greater detail and send out a final bid.

Combing through projects in the CFBE taught me a lot. It was critically important to make accurate analysis of the time and materials needed to submit a bid. A bid had to be fair, accurate, high enough to make a profit, and low enough to beat out the competition. It was even more of a challenge since we were the new kids on the block. Because Tri-City was relatively unknown, gaining the trust of reputable contactors was the Holy Grail for our business.

Once we were awarded a contract, the highest goal was to complete the project on time and within budget. If we operated with a short-term mentality and went for profits only, I doubt we would have lasted. It all came down to how accurately we estimated each and every project. If I underestimated material cost or labor, I simply ate the loss, pressed on, and did a better job the next time.

So, we put in our bids again and again, and over time we achieved a fairly decent closure rate on what we submitted. Hard work and consistency began to pay off in terms of reputation and repeat business.

There was another thing I believe helped us grow: I always treated everyone the best I could. I honestly tried to do that without fail and to the best of my ability. Whatever I said I intended to do, I did. I never defaulted on a job, and if it required more help than what we had, we worked on the weekends or later at night, whatever it took to get it done.

Apparently, we were doing things right because referrals began to ease the load of sorting through all those bid requests. It's a well-known fact that referral business is far cheaper than advertising, and it also meant our status had gained some traction in the marketplace. So, it looked like we'd earned the reputation as a company in business to stay, and one that could handle reasonably large jobs. To land serious jobs from general contractors, they had to know we could deliver; that we weren't some "small potatoes" company trying to break into the big time.

One of our first major commercial jobs came in our fifth year, and we landed it with the help of the CFBE. The general contractor was Henry Stevens of the H. B. Stephens Construction Company out of Orlando, who was building a small office on Morse Boulevard in Winter Park, near our office. The building would be the headquarters of Lanier Business Systems, which sold and serviced 3M copy machines among other things. Compared with today's special electrical applications, such as security systems or "smart environments," the Lanier contract was a plain vanilla commercial wiring job. But it was big enough for me.

I already had several electricians working at Tri-City, so we were geared up for the project. The structure would have 4,536-square-feet of enclosed area, and the electrical contract was right at $50,000, a healthy amount for 1963. I'm proud to say we completed the job on time and on budget.

The years passed, and we continued to forge new clients in an ever-widening area from Altamonte Springs. The workload increased as well, so we created company divisions: residential, multi-family, apartment house, and commercial. Each division had an overseer. In addition to managing the residential division, Fred Kroker oversaw the residential estimating department and continued to perform estimates himself. One of his helpers, Rance Borderick, was hired right out of high school, and he worked his way up to become our multi-family and residential project manager. Today, Rance is one of our vice presidents and one of the owners of Tri-City. He also holds our Florida state electrical license.

Along with increased projects came an increasing number of purchasing needs. Every project demanded certain types of supplies with exact specifications, to be delivered in specific amounts to the right place. The accounting requirements to keep track of all that mounted as well, sometimes creating headaches for those who oversaw that task. I don't know what we would have done without the help of Bob Rudolph, my brother-in-law, who helped us immensely by creating a purchasing system with accurate, blanket pricing for our suppliers. Once that was in place, we breathed a little easier.

Just a Couple of Young Guys

I worked for an electrical supply distributor named Hughes Supply since late 1955, starting out as a delivery driver. One of the first deliveries I made was to Buddy Eidel in 1959, at a place on the corner of Dog Track Road and Route 1792. That happened to be the home of Mr. Charles Eidel, Buddy's father. I got to know Buddy fairly well since both of us were just "young kids" at the time. His order was for ten boxes of Romex wire along with other supplies. After Buddy bought his first home, I continued to deliver Romex, but I dropped them off in his carport. Buddy had just bought a used truck from the telephone company, his first company vehicle.

I worked up through the ranks at Hughes, and Buddy kept expanding and growing his business as well. The Hughes brothers didn't realize at the time that we would grow right along with our customers, so as we all expanded, our continuing business and relationship with Tri-City expanded as well.

I stayed with Hughes for thirty-five years and retired as Executive V.P. of the company. Throughout that time, Buddy and I have remained good friends. We were both involved in Associated Builders and Contractors (a national trade association, also known as ABC) in the Central Florida chapter where Buddy was president for a while. I was its twenty-fifth president, and we also belong to the same Interlachen Golf Club in Winter Park.

When I first met Buddy, I thought he was just a hard-working young guy who wanted to go places. As time went on, he kept working harder and he got smarter. He also hired some very good people in the industry along the way.

At one time, Tri-City had a reputation of taking work too cheaply. But Buddy just was more efficient at his work. That's how he made money. Today, his company is one of the largest of its kind in Florida.

I remember an event that happened a long time ago, and it said a lot about Buddy. There was a contactor in the industry who was a real blowhard. I'll call him "Jack B." One time, Buddy was working on a job and Jack ordered someone to fill in a ditch that Buddy was still working in. That made Buddy angry because he wasn't finished with the job. Well, Buddy isn't very tall in stature, but he went out to the site and backed that blowhard contractor right down to size. I'm not sure what he said, but apparently it worked. Everybody in the industry thought that was the greatest thing.

In terms of our industry, Tri-City and Buddy really championed the apprentice training programs. The training was originally administered through ABC, but Buddy, with others at Tri-City, boosted the program and elevated the professionalism of the electrical industry in the state.

Bill Weir - Executive Vice-President, Hughes Electric Supply (Retired)

Buddy working at home on blueprints 1970

11

The Best Kind of Model

Most companies our size had business development people, but we waited quite a while before we hired our own. That had been my responsibility from day one, and it seemed to work fairly well, so I kept it up. But, I believe most of our success was due to word of mouth; by simply doing a good job. On our fiftieth anniversary, my friend Bill Harkins remarked: "As Buddy often said, "You know, if I told somebody I was going to do it, I was going to damn well make it happen."

When we experienced periods of rapid growth, it tended to shake my dad up. But he hung in there and tempered me somewhat, which was good. For example, when an expansion called for buying more trucks or equipment (too many to dad's thinking), he was a good sounding board, right along with my mom. They were Germans who came through the Depression and saw hard times, so they were pretty frugal. Their perspective helped me a lot, particularly when it came to making decisions on sizeable expenditures. One time I displayed light fixtures in our storefront. What I thought was a great idea really bombed, and all dad could do was shake his head.

On the other side of the spectrum, when we hit a downturn (which happens regularly in our industry) we always did our best to keep our people busy. During one particularly slow period, I sent a couple of our electricians to our home. Paula and I lived in Quail Hollow and we had a long fence that needed painting, so we gave the job to our guys instead of outsourcing it to someone outside of the family. We got our fence painted, and they stayed on the payroll.

Dad got involved too. He always had something that needed to be painted or repaired at their motel property or at his own house, so he used Tri-City employees. We always did our best, because our most precious asset in the business was our people.

As I look back on those times, I realize how thankful I am for my dad, both of my parents in fact, but dad in particular. He toiled so hard and long to take care of us after we arrived in Florida; he was the role model that shaped my work ethic. Back in 1948, when there was nothing but orange groves and pastureland in this area, it was extremely hard to scratch out a living. But he and mom made it work. Later, when I decided to go out on my own, it was dad's hard work and faith in me that led him to take the risks he did. After he finished his day job, he helped me wire houses in the evenings and weekends. He kept that up until the business took on a life of its own and I could hire additional help.

12

Our First Big One

By the time we reached our ninth year, we'd expanded significantly into the commercial side of the business around Orlando. The Lanier project helped us get our feet wet, and now it was time for the next big job.

Our foray into our next seriously large contract was for a new car dealership , McNamara Pontiac. McNamara was well known and respected in Central Florida, and when I heard about the pending project on Highway 50 and U.S. 441, I went for it. What I believe helped the process was David Beasley, one of my electricians and the son of a superintendent at Jack Jennings & Sons general contractors. After David joined our company, he wired apartments with Bill Duym at our first project for Earl Downs Construction. I felt that every connection, however small, would help us through the bidding process.

In the years running up to McNamara, we managed to forge a good relationship with Jennings, mostly through contracting for various projects. I always treated them fairly and honestly, and always came through on what I said I would do. They in turn did the same for us. Such are the basic ingredients of a long-term, successful relationship, whether personal or business.

We made what I thought was a fair, aggressive offer for McNamara. After I submitted it, low and behold we were the lowest bidder, significantly lower. Although we already had twenty employees at Tri-City, I had to hire another dozen electricians for the project. Most of them were from the same pool we had used for previous jobs, which helped eliminate the guesswork.

The project lasted eighteen months from start to finish. Like any construction job, there were challenges along the way, but we worked them out and went on to do more work for the Jennings Company.

In a sense, fulfilling the contract for McNamara was only part of the job. It was a huge learning process for Tri-City. It stood to reason that landing, and successfully completing, a big job like that revealed some practices we needed to improve if we wanted to continue. We learned right away that we needed to increase our capacity in all areas of the business. But the really big lesson was to correctly interpret the bidding documents. Accurate bidding. I had made a major error that could have sunk our business.

I mentioned earlier that we were the lowest bidder, and there was a reason. I submitted our estimate based on what I thought was the entire project. But I inadvertently left out one of the adjacent buildings earmarked for their used car sales office. It was supposed to be a deductive alternate — an alternate bid resulting in a deduction from our base bid — but it should have been factored into our initial offer. The fact that I left that building out of my offer went unnoticed until after we were well underway with the project. Tri-City ended up giving them a credit, and we had to wire the building anyway! It cost us a lot, but it didn't inflict permanent damage. In the end, my omission turned out to be a kind of benediction for the big leagues in electrical contracting.

After that inadvertent low bid, we were far more careful. I became more aware of what could go wrong and adopted the phrase: "Let's not work harder, let's work smarter." While that phrase is simple and obvious, it affected our bottom line: to make real money in a highly competitive bid arena, we had to work very smart. We could not put extra profit in a job to make up for errors, so most of the jobs awarded to us were because we bid the lowest. So, to make it work, I had to structure the business as efficiently possible. I began to realize that we could only make money by being accurate *and* efficient.

Creating a more accurate estimating program was a real learning curve. It took a long time, but I eventually developed a system that broke down jobs by area and work products, down to the lowest common denominator. We tracked how long it took to run conduit, pull wire, and install outlets for every unit and any eventuality. Only when we could nail down those essentials could we be truly competitive.

The McNamara project also taught us not to bite off more than we could chew. Every organization wants to reach higher to land the venture, but a company can be severely burned if it exceeds its capacity to fufill the project. I didn't want to go there, so I tried to keep our company within our level of competency until we could grow into bigger projects. McNamara was a fairly big job at the time, and the scope was almost more than we could handle. But we worked out butts off and made it through.

I also applied another principle: I decided to work on becoming more efficient with our profit margins, rather than build extra profit into our jobs. That meant our profitability would not come from the top end, but from efficiencies. Simply put, do better with less. That's how we could offer lower bids and still maintain our margins.

In that vein, I learned a valuable maxim at a management seminar that goes, "Profit thrills, but revenue kills." My interpretation was, "More revenue is not always in the best interest of the company. Sound profit margins are."

***

The long hours of sweating in a CBFE plan room or at night in our home office with pencils, erasers, calculators, and copious amounts of coffee are long gone. Technology does most of the grunt work now through computers and CAD (computer-aided design) systems. Coming from the pre-technology era to the present, I'm amazed at how things have changed. Fortunately, through hiring bright, hard working people, Tri-City has kept up with the pace of technology and stayed strong in the face of competition.

The Systems Guy

Buddy wrote the company's basic estimating program, but he admits he didn't know what he was doing and was flying by the seat of his pants. The program was very sophomoric, but at least the system worked and it gave them something to move ahead with. He eventually found a professional company in Maryland to write a much slicker program. Ever since, Buddy has been all about doing things better than anybody else, as long as we had a system in place.

So, he's a real systems guy, but not just with programs. We keep huge notebooks for each department detailing how that department works, who does what, and who is responsible. It's amazing to me, and to be honest, I thought it was a huge waste of time. So, I wasn't totally enthusiastic. I thought, "Oh my God, I have to put all those notebooks together and I really don't want to because nobody will use it." But now I see the effectiveness of them, and how a new employee can know what the previous employee did. We improved on the system every year, and now I can see how farsighted those books were.

Paula Eidel

13

Hard, Consistent Work

My parents continued to support our company. Mom still kept the books, and dad kept pace with the business. Later on, he became passionate about safety in the company. Maybe it came from his youth, when he worked for a bus company and was run over by a bus that messed up his leg. As a result, he had a slight limp for the rest of his life. Whatever the reason, dad's mission to improve the safety and well-being of the employees turned into the position of safety director for Tri-City. His concern for safety spread throughout the company until the employees affectionately referred to him as "Papa Eidel." They all loved him. Today, a sign reflecting his concern for workers is painted on the inside wall of the Charles J. Eidel Training Building in his endearing German accent:

"I can always buy a ladder, I can no' replace a man."

Charles J. "Papa" Eidel

Dad often went out on jobs to check on safety, and in so doing became our best ambassador. There were many times I couldn't get out to the projects as much as I should have, since employees always like to see management on the job. I was busy trying to grow the company, so dad filled in.

During our engagement with the McNamara project, dad acquired an additional hat in the company. He became Tri-City's official "money collector," not only from Jennings, but other contractors, too. He got along very well with Jack Jennings (Tony's father). When it was time to get paid for our subcontracting work, dad drove to their office and collected the money. When the official business was over, and if Jack was in, dad dropped by his office for a chat. We were convinced the

Buddy and the Gorilla

Buddy and Papa

two of them solved most of the ills of the construction industry during those sessions.

***

When the McNamara project was done, and the client was pleased and we were paid, I could finally say our business was a success. Another tangible measure of that success was moving away from the required personal guarantees with the bank and bonding company. In reality, I knew we were successful for quite some time, but I didn't think we were really *done*. That would happen many years later, when we finally got off the personal guarantees. In the meantime, we had to keep going, growing, getting better, and staying strong. In a sense, Tri-City's situation fit the words on a poster I saw at the time: "When you're dancing with a gorilla you can never quit."

"Buddy Bucks"

I first met Buddy Eidel around 1980, when my brother and I graduated from the University of Florida. We met Buddy and his wife, Paula, at an ABC event. Our dad, Jack Jennings, helped found the Orlando chapter along with Buddy, and it was around that time we all got to know each other. In fact, the ABC is where many of us still meet and keep in touch, because ABC is a central part of our community.

I would describe Buddy as a kind, soft spoken, non-intimidating individual. He had such a nice demeanor, always wore a smile, and seemed to have a very positive outlook on life, a real can-do attitude. Frankly, I never saw anything negative about him. He really was a good soul, trying to do a good job for the employees.

Most couples have a hard time working and living together 24/7, but Paula really pitched in and helped the company grow. The two of them simply worked well together and I don't know of any other husband and wife combination in our industry quite like that.

In my estimation, nearly every major building in downtown Orlando has Tri-City's name on it. The convention center, the airport, the arena — all those projects and many more were done by Tri-City.

I have to mention Mr. Eidel Senior, or Charles as he was known here. Since we were the general contractor, Charles used to come to our office to pick up Tri-City's check, and that's how I first came to know him. Charles and my dad would usually get together in his office and chat about the industry and life in general.

Buddy was involved in many community organizations, and although he was often behind the scenes, he was an extremely effective leader.

A key event in the early days was their first job with us at McNamara Pontiac, and as of today, we have five ongoing jobs with Tri-City worth about $20 million. Over the past forty years, I can say Tri-City has done more than 75 percent of our electrical work. Today, there are three generations of Jennings in Jack Jennings & Sons. We now have a third generation on board; my two sons and my brother's kids as well. So, it looks like the relationship between our two companies will go on and on.

I'll always remember something Buddy did for public relations: it was a gimmick called "Buddy Bucks." They were green dollar bills that looked somewhat like the real thing, except Buddy's photo was in the spot normally occupied by George Washington. Tri-City sent them out to all their partners in the industry, and we got a bunch of them. Sometime later, when my brother met up with Buddy, he pulled a Buddy Bucks bill out of his wallet and asked him to sign it. I imagine that was a brainchild of his wife, Paula.

Jeff Jennings, of Jack Jennings & Sons Construction Services

14

Innovate and Grow

After McNamara, we concentrated more on the commercial side of the business. And every time we completed a new commercial job, we wound up taking care of their electrical service needs down the road. The reason is after our initial contract, the customer might expand their facilities or upgrade their systems. And since we installed it in the first place, and they liked our work, we were the ones they called to do the maintenance or upgrades. Due to McNamara, we were able to contract with several of the other car dealerships in the area, and soon it became kind of our niche. Some examples are Johnny Bolton Ford Company in Maitland, and the Lewis Motors out on Highway 50. One thing just led to another, and the business grew.

As we grew, we needed to make our estimating even more efficient. It was extremely time consuming to narrow prospect data down to that sweet spot where we could bid low but still make money. The fact was, we only landed about 25 percent of all the work we bid on, which made accurate estimating even more important. And due to the constant fluctuation of the economy, our bids varied in terms of overall cost and margin. When the economy (and usually our industry) got tight, we had to shave our margins as much as possible to remain competitive. Occasionally our percentages dropped too low, and other electrical contractors threw out equally low, or even lower, bids. There were instances when we wound up with jobs that actually lost money. Such was the price to pay to remain in the game.

I came to realize that if we were going to carve out as much margin as possible while remaining the low bidder, we needed a customized computerized estimating system. These programs began to show up in the market about that time, but when I checked them out closely, I felt I could do a better job. We already had an in-house computer programmer, and after he studied the other applications on the market, he came up with one that suited our needs. My job was to inject the parameters, the numbers, assemblies, and other data, to the system. An example of an assembly is when the plan calls for a certain number of electrical receptacles with a box, it will require a plaster ring for the receptacle and the installation of a faceplate. Then I bundled it into an assembly and gave it a specific code. That, plus thousands of other assemblies, went into the estimating system and it vastly improved the process. Details like that added to our costs, which in turn affected our offering price. All these details were important to me, and so I spent untold numbers of hours trying to make the system work better.

Paula used to tease me about my crazy work schedule. Sometimes we went to the beach and while she was swimming or playing with the kids, I'd sit under an umbrella going over a pile of paperwork. I figured out the assemblies and assigned each assembly a part number for our programmer so he could do his job. I felt an urgency about everything, so although I was present on the white sand, my mind was on developing programs to take us to the next level of efficiency.

Honestly, the new estimating program was crude, but it was also quite successful. We used it four or five years until eventually, after the technology improved, we bought one of the mainline programs. It covered a lot more ground than our original one, and allowed us to tweak, or customize, our system to be even more efficient.

On Diversity

From the start, Tri-City never had a specific "diversity program." Throughout the life of the company, we were always color, ethnic, religious, and gender blind. We just looked for the best, most qualified person for a job and that was that. I also believe we were one of the first companies to hire female apprentices to work in the field. One of the first things our apprentices learned was how to use a skill saw for roughing in an apartment for electrical work. Now that was progress!

Buddy

15

FAEC and NECA

Aside from dad, another person stands out as one who helped me in the early years. His name was Howard Palmer, owner of Palmer Electric Company in Winter Park. Howard believed that an educated competitor was better than an uneducated competitor who didn't know their costs or how to estimate their work. In his thinking, a savvy competitor was a known, or predictable entity that would bid within logical margins.

FAEC Awards Banquet – 1973

That was far better than an unwise competitor who might unwittingly lowball a bid and knock everyone else out of the running, only to wind up with massive cost overruns. This led Howard to be very active in a trade association named FAEC, or Florida Association of Electrical Contractors. FAEC was sort of a nonunion version of NECA (National Electrical Contractors of America).

FAEC members were electrical contractors who wanted to boost their industry, and therefore their own business, throughout the state. To that end, the association developed training seminars for electrical code and other business-related topics. Those and other programs supplemented their usual monthly meetings, and as a result, members became stronger competitors. That was important because FAEC was a nonunion association that avoided labor issues. Members came from Jacksonville, Tallahassee, Miami, and throughout Florida's West Coast.

Howard, along with co-members Wally and Axel Ornberg, Floyd Clark, Jim Ward, and Wes Olson, were instrumental in starting the Florida State Electrical Licensing Board. Until then, electricians had to go to places like Winter Park or Tampa to take the journeyman or master's exam to get licensed in every city where they planned to work. All the time and travel required became a real burden. But it wasn't just FAEC's problem: every electrical worker in the state had to comply, union and nonunion. With the FAEC taking the lead, companies like Paxon Electric, Miller Electric Company, and other members of NECA (a union association) jumped in to help the initiative.

Eventually the licensing initiative went to the state legislature, which voted it into law. Today, the construction licensing board works within the bailiwick of the Florida construction industry. Getting the licensing initiative passed was a big deal back then, and when it was over everyone's workload became a bit easier.

Tri-City joined FAEC in 1963 because we felt the need to be part of an organization that supported our industry. Dad and I often attended the local meetings and witnessed a lot of good come from the educational materials they developed. Mingling with others in our industry also let

Paula and Buddy at Barbecue - Date unknown

me in on some of their best business practices, which helped me take a closer look at the way Tri-City did things. It helped verify the good training I received from the union-sponsored apprenticeship program in my earlier years, and the technical knowledge that came with it. I was like a sponge, absorbing all the knowledge I could. Then one year, lo and behold, they elected me president of the association!

During that period, we were also members of NECA when they still allowed nonunion members. We worked closely with the local NECA chapter president, Doug Hayes, while he tried to make peace between union and nonunion contractors. We remained with NECA until they introduced a new membership fee based on a percentage of annual income. Our dues grew so quickly that it was no longer feasible to stay with the association. Again, Doug tried to smooth that out, but in the end, we had to leave.

Despite the changes, I take my hat off to NECA because they developed excellent educational materials and their labor unit manual has become a standard for the electrical industry. The manual is used industry wide to determine fair pricing for change orders, and how to cost electrical work. Not surprisingly, we used NECA's materials as a springboard for our own training.

**

As Florida's economy continued to build steam, and NASA and the new Disney World came along, our local economy continued its upward trend. It was only natural that competitive businesses would occasionally bump into one another, but we got around those events. Except for the occasional economic downturn, all electrical contractor boats rose with the tide. The industry grew, became more professional, and prospered.

Unfortunately, a few bad apples took it upon themselves to disrupt others who played fair in our free enterprise system. That includes the arsonist who acted out his frustrations in 1971 and burned down our office and warehouse on Robin Road in Altamonte Springs. It took a long time and a lot of effort to rebuild after that.

On a positive note, a woman named Paula joined the company.

II
TOWARD HIGHER GROUND

1

Paula's Story

My maiden name is *Distelhourst*. As you can imagine, I hated it, mostly because no one knew how to spell it. As I made my way through school, I swore that I'd marry a Smith or a Jones so I wouldn't have to spell it out to people all the time. So what happened? I married an *Eidel*, so of course everyone spelled it "idol."

My Distelhourst parents were fourth-generation German-American, and they raised me and my three siblings with what I call a "fifties mentality." Actually, that wasn't so much out of the norm because about one-fourth of the Indiana population claimed German descent. Mother was a stay-at-home mom and my dad was the breadwinner, so the atmosphere was strict, conservative German. Like every family, we had our little dysfunctions, but overall I loved my upbringing and I have no complaints.

As a family, we enjoyed traditional holidays and get-togethers, and throughout school I had tons of friends. My mother always said she'd rather we bring our friends to our house instead of somewhere else so she could keep an eye on things. And to help us stay on track, she hosted chili parties during basketball season when our friends were always welcome. Things like that. On school days, Mother would leave the back door open because she was president of the PTA and often stayed late at the meetings. She'd tell me she wouldn't be home until five, and to come through the back door and get myself a snack before starting homework. We lived in the same the neighborhood for twenty years, so I knew everybody and it was always safe. It saddens me that it's no longer all that safe.

My grandmother Fetzer, on my dad's side of the family, was a member of the Scott Fetzer Co. of Cleveland, Ohio. They produced and sold Kirby vacuum cleaners, and my grandfather owned the Kirby distributorship in Toledo. The family business was what influenced my dad to become a vacuum cleaner salesman. So he did, and he was quite good at it. He got so good, he could sell you the shirt off his back.

After several years in the business, dad moved our family to Indianapolis to establish his own Kirby distributorship. The business thrived, and when we were old enough, my siblings and I had to work at the business. Honestly, we all absolutely hated it, mostly because it seemed like dad was meaner to us than to anyone else in the office. That was probably because we were his kids and he didn't want to show favoritism. When it came to his work ethic, it seemed like my father went at his job just as hard as Buddy, but he somehow managed to get home by 5:30 p.m. every night. So, dad worked hard most of the time. But then there was race week.

The Indianapolis 500 car race had been around since 1911, so race week was a big deal for us. Every year dad would roast a pig in the backyard for the event and invite the entire neighborhood. Later in the summer, my siblings and I would ride our bikes to the Riviera Swim Club and stay there all day. Mom gave us fifty cents each for a drink and a hot dog, and we were out the door by 8:30 a.m. We usually got home around five, all tired and burned to a crisp.

My family was conservative, much like Buddy's. When I was sixteen, I wanted to buy a special dress for the prom. I found it in a downtown department store and it was beautiful, with white lace and sequins. But it cost $100, which was an outrageous price in the fifties, even if my dad made a good living. But I still wanted that dress more than anything, and told Dad I was willing to pay for half of it. When he said yes, I went right to work. I babysat. I mowed lawns. I did everything I could do to earn fifty bucks, sometimes a quarter at a time. But I did it. I earned the money and we bought that dress.

2

Many Roles

I was an educated, trained administrative assistant (a nice title for secretary), and I scoured all the want ads in all the local papers around the Orlando area. I didn't want to pay some referral service to find a job for me, so I went from ad to ad making phone calls, believing my verbal skills on the phone might convince someone to ask me in for an interview. That's how it was in the late sixties and early seventies. When I saw the opening at Tri-City I was intrigued. First, it wasn't in downtown Orlando. Second, it was a convenient distance for me. So, I asked for an interview. They said yes, and that's how I landed the job.

I mainly worked as an accountant for Buddy's brother, Charles, but I also did a bit of everything else for a number of managers. One day Charles asked me to write a letter to one of their contractors about a money issue. I typed it up and gave it to him. When he looked at it he muttered, "Oh my God, I've never had a letter like this before." I didn't think it was that unusual, but apparently it was new to him and he loved it. Since then, I took care of most of his correspondence as well as everything else. Before I knew it, several other managers wanted me to type their letters, including the owner, Buddy Eidel.

My first conversation with Buddy took place at the company Christmas party in 1971. I immediately got the impression that he was a very nice man. I wasn't used to anybody being that nice, particularly someone in charge of a large company. I can't say I immediately fell head over heels in love with him, but I did think, "Wow, this guy is unique and

Buddy & Paula on trip to Jamaica – around 1975

TCE employees at Christmas – date unknown

I like him!" I still do, but by then I was all grown up and realized marriage wasn't just all about romance. We just seemed like kindred spirits. While there was always romance in our life, we became best friends and soul mates as well.

We really complimented one another: I had a little more formal education mixed with Indiana sophistication, and he was a kind, "good ole boy" from the South with the vision and foresight to build a highly successful business. He started by wiring houses as an electrician, and had a strong desire to learn and grow. Together, we made a great team.

After we married, I moved over to his end of the building and became his full-time secretary. When I wasn't doing secretarial work, I took care of our personal finances, paid our bills, and kept the household running so he wouldn't have to worry about it. Sometimes he'd come to me and ask if we had any money because he was out. That kind of arrangement kept him free to do the more important things.

There is another side of our life that must be told. We both had been previously married at a young age, and because of that those relationships had failed. So, when we met in our early thirties, we felt stronger, wiser, and more capable of creating a successful marriage and to raise and nurture our blended family of five children. Our children were not always happy, and there were many challenges. But we liked and respected one another, and were determined to make it work.

3

Caring for Two Families

When I joined Tri-City we had eight other women working for us. As a woman I could see there were certain things they needed that weren't being taken care of by the company. For example, the company's maternity leave policy allowed a maximum of only six weeks. I told Buddy women needed more than that because as a woman, I would have a hard time going back to work so soon after giving birth. Women become so connected to their newborn child that all they'll do is worry about that baby at home. It made no sense for a woman to be so emotionally conflicted that she couldn't do her job. I suggested we give our female employees at least three months off, twice the current allotment, for maternity leave with a guarantee their job would be there when they returned. Buddy did it, but after the policy changed a couple of women still came back after six weeks. Eventually, the rest of them took all three months. This was a great morale booster for our staff.

Early on, I helped some of the managers with their correspondence. But over time it developed into the marketing end of the business, which included boosting employee morale. I realized employees love to see their name in print, along with photos of them receiving an award with a handshake from managers. So, one day I suggested we start a company newspaper. That way we could highlight the accomplishments of as many employees as possible. When Buddy gave me the green light, I went right to work. We called it the *WattsLine*.

I printed the early issues on one of those old Gestetner mimeograph machines, those cumbersome things that made a lot of noise and smelled like a gas station. It was hard work, and printing a two or three-page newsletter for a hundred employees took a lot of time. But it was necessary to communicate with everyone at every level of the company, and I wanted to include as many employees as I could in every issue to highlight what they'd accomplished. I announced marriages, births, and heralded the awards they received for safety or other achievements. As soon as the *WattsLine* was up and going, other tasks began to emerge. I was involved in organizing our Christmas parties and our company picnics. I filled in wherever I could to increase the sense of family.

On Hard Work

Call it my German roots, but I learned early on that anything worth having in life would take a lot of hard work. But there's a balance to that: I also

---

> preached work smarter, not harder. The combination
> of the two, hard and smart, takes effort. But in the
> long run it proved to be the best, most competitive
> force I know of. I always tried to set an example by
> working side-by-side with all our managers, putting
> in the time required to get the job done right. This is
> a simple philosophy, but it works every time.
>
> **Buddy**

Not long after Buddy and I married, one of our hires, Bob Veazey, came on board as an electrician at our Atlantic Drive location. Soon, Buddy saw his potential and asked him to come into the office to start estimating. Buddy and Bob spent about a year studying for the Florida license exam, and they wound up taking it together. It was a very difficult exam, but on December 6, 1974, they both passed on the first try. Buddy's assigned license number was 226, which placed him among the state board's first few hundred license holders. When Tri-City was licensed statewide, instead of in several local counties, it opened doors to work around the rest of the state. That was the start of a tremendous surge of growth.

4

Create the Vision

For many, many years, Tri-City struggled to get people interest in an electrical career because it involved labor and training. All the construction trades faced the same challenge of acquiring and keeping qualified labor to build our buildings, bridges, roads, and everything else. Not everyone can go to college and become a doctor, a lawyer, or an Indian chief.

During the fifties in Indiana, the number of people with a college degree was very low, but I was fortunate to have graduated from a college preparatory school in Indianapolis. It was fairly unusual for poor people to go to college: young women got married right out of high school and the men went to a trade school for carpentry, plumbing, electrical, and auto mechanic training. Those were considered respectable jobs back then, but the general opinion seems to have changed.

After a while at Tri-City, I came to believe that the public needed to look again and realize those jobs were respectable, even if workers had to get a bit dirty now and then. Entering one of the trades should be right up there in priority with other professions. That's why Tri-City focused on training very early on, and that's why Buddy kept wages and benefits as high as he could. As he often said, "Don't try to pay your employee as little as possible, but as much as possible."

The problem is, very few people want to dig ditches in Florida, or anywhere else for that matter. But if anyone wanted to become an electrician, they had to start out doing just that. The ditch digging part is actually short-term, and if they went to electrician's school for two or three years in the meantime, they could become a journeyman. Then they'd have one of the highest paying jobs in the trade.

Everyone in a management position at Tri-City started out digging ditches in the hot Florida sun. From there they climbed up the chain, if they wanted to. We always tried to promote from within and sent some employees to apprenticeship school, or to college. We did everything we could to encourage our people to improve themselves. The more they improved, the more our company improved. It didn't matter how many jobs we had or how long our backlog was, our greatest asset were the electricians, not management. Still, the message about all the positives of the electrical trade was lost on many, particularly young people. So, I decided to get out there and spread the word to middle and high school students.

I told Buddy I wanted to start a campaign to reach high schoolers with that message, and he said he was okay with it. Everybody else at the company was too busy, and I didn't think the associations or other organizations had done enough to get the word out to young people.

I began by visiting junior high schools, to pique their interest while they were young and impressionable. I started with the Orange County Public Schools and at Glenridge Junior High, because my children attended that school and I knew a lot of the faculty. I visited their classrooms and talked with the seventh and eighth graders.

My message went something like this: "Hey kids. If you can't afford to, or don't want to, go to college there's an alternative. And it's not a dead-end job like selling drugs or flipping hamburgers." I wanted them to know the electrical trade is respectable and that electricians make a good living with great benefits. They could be the ones to help build skyscrapers, bridges, arenas, and roads we see all over the place.

I tried to get them excited by relating Buddy's story, which is a good one. I said that if Buddy can make millions, why couldn't they? I tried to convince kids to consider a path toward trade school instead of college because I knew they weren't all going to college. I kept knocking on school doors and I kept talking.

Who knows if my talks had any effect? When it comes to kids that age, it's often hard to tell if they're really listening. All I could do was hope my words took root in some of those young minds and maybe a few of them are working at Tri-City right now.

5

You Can Lead Them to Water

Buddy did not want to be a member of a union. However, he knew that if we wanted to keep our employees, we'd have to provide health insurance just like the unions. The difference was, union employees got benefits by paying a lot of monthly dues for them. Buddy thought that was ridiculous and decided to provide our employees with health insurance anyway. We did, and we were the first in our area to do so.

Once they had health insurance, we decided to extend family insurance coverage as well. Then we put together a 401 (k) retirement savings program, but when we rolled out the offer, it was like pulling teeth. Convincing employees it was a good deal was challenging because in those days employees in general were not very sophisticated. When payday came, many of them went out and bought beer and cigarettes, and most of them didn't save a dime throughout their working life. Also, the concept of a 401 (k) was new, and very foreign to them. We kept stressing that they should set some money aside, but it wasn't in their thought process. We finally used the best incentive out there — free money.

We held investment seminars at our office and offered them $100 just to attend. That's what it took to get them to listen to what a great deal the program could be. We said we'd match their investment with twenty-five cents on the dollar, explaining they would make 25 percent on their money immediately. But most of them still didn't understand, or they thought it would take too much time to build up any significant savings. They were young, and as youth go they simply didn't care much beyond the upcoming weekend.

It was interesting when my daughter, who is a physician, first went to work she called Buddy and told him they had a 401 (k). She said they wanted her to put X-amount of dollars in the program, and asked him if she should do it. Of course, Buddy said, "Yes, yes, and yes again!"

Tri-City's program was, and still is, a very good one and it supplemented our equally generous bonus program. We even published our 401(k) numbers in the *WattsLine* for all to see. Of course, as Tri-City grew, so did the employees' investments. If a bad year rolled in, we had to tell them there was no matching funds for that year. In fact, one year was so bad we sent our best electricians out to our house to paint the fence just to keep them busy. They needed a dignified reason for their paycheck instead of a handout.

In 2017, the company continued the legacy of providing great benefits by establishing an ESOP, or Employee Stock Ownership Plan, whereby the ownership of the company was transferred in part to the employees over time.

Leadfoot

I have been with Tri-City since 1979, when they were still on Atlantic Avenue. They hired me to work a backhoe, run some equipment, and do mechanic work. At first, I worked out of a shed in a corner of the parking lot, and after a while I asked if they'd build a better place for me. The bosses said yes, and I put up a metal building with enough space for a desk and a chair. The culture at Tri-City is unique.

Buddy, Paula, and Papa Eidel thought that as long as you did your job, you were treated equally. You wouldn't know Buddy owned the place because he treated you with respect, like part of the family. In fact, they were all that way.

When my wife, Linda, first came into my life, I wanted to take her on an official date. But my car was real ratty so I asked Paula if I could use their new, white, Chrysler Fifth Avenue for the event. Paula said yes, and apparently it worked because we got married.

Papa Eidel really liked my wife and me, and when he got on in years, he'd sometimes call me up to join him for breakfast or dinner. If it was dinner, he'd tell me to bring Linda along because she didn't drink and we needed a driver to get us home after a few highballs.

Then there was Papa's pontoon boat. He was fairly old when he got it, and one day he decided to move it to the St. John's River near where he lived. The deal was he couldn't take it out unless either our friend, Charlie Prendergast, or I went with him. So that's what Papa did: he'd call on Saturday morning asking if we all could go for a ride.

Buddy was driven to succeed for sure, and I've never seen anyone work like him. But he was always fair. One time he called us all together and said, "We're going to have to cut hours and jobs, but if you stay with me, I'll do the best I can and make it up to you when things get better." He did, and he always stood by his word.

On the other hand, you don't want to be on his wrong side because that German temperament might come right out. I was at his desk one time when the conversation got a little heated when I made a comment that hit him the wrong way. He hit the ceiling so to speak, but when it was over we went right back to business. I actually thought I'd get fired for it, but he called me to his office and said, "okay, we're good now, aren't we?"

One time we thought about placing GPS software in the company cars to monitor speed and mileage, so I installed test systems in some of the cars, including Buddy's. Buddy had a reputation for having a heavy right foot, and when certain people noted his GPS recording of 93 miles an hour, he told me to take it out of his car.

Buddy in the Atlantic Drive office – 1976

> The Eidels were good to me and Tri-City was good to me. That's why I stayed until I retired and can now do what my wife and I are doing at the age of sixty-two, which is to roam the American West in our R.V.
>
> **Bruce Beane, Retired Fleet Manager**

6

Off to Harvard

One morning during breakfast, Buddy looked across the table at me and remarked, "You know what? I think by the end of the year we're going to do $10 million in business." When he said that, I have to admit it scared me. But that's exactly what we did, with help from the Harvard Business School. It all began with the owner of a beer distributorship named Jim Taylor.

Jim's business was next door to ours and he and Buddy were good friends. One day Jim came by our office and dropped off a brochure for Buddy to look at. It was about a program offered at Harvard called the SCMP, Smaller Company Management Program. Years later, it changed to the OPMP, Owner and President Management Program. Regardless of the name, it was designed for emerging companies like Tri-City. Jim said he just finished the program and thought it would be the perfect thing for Buddy since he and a few others had discussed the need to take Tri-City to the next level. Here was the gist of the brochure:

> "Building and running a successful company can be an all-consuming challenge that leaves little time for business owners to focus on their personal growth. That means candidates must be fully equipped to master a range of skills

— from strategy development to financial management to team building to negotiation.

The Owner/President Management program provides a transformative and supportive environment where they can step back from daily operations and learn how to become a more effective leader, deliver greater value to stakeholders, and ensure further success for themselves and their companies.

Designed with business owners and entrepreneurs in mind, OPM is ideal for owners/founders with at least ten years of work experience who also serve as chief executive officers, chief operating officers, presidents, managing directors, or executive directors of companies with annual revenues or established enterprise value in excess of $10 million. In addition to being actively involved in running the business, candidates must hold a significant equity stake in their firms."

After Buddy read the brochure and talked more with Jim, he knew the course was exactly what he needed. That's where his comment over breakfast about $10 million in revenues came from. The program called for three weeks on campus each summer over a three-year period for a total of nine weeks. The group would work from Harvard case studies of actual businesses, and simulate a company scenario where they would act as leaders of that corporation.

To get into the program, participants were required to have an up and going, relatively successful business. Formal education wasn't an issue because Harvard understood many successful entrepreneurs lacked higher education, and some never even finished high school. To their thinking, a "successful business" meant a turnover of around $10 million. We were almost there, so we enrolled in the school that would start in the summer of 1980.

When I said "we" enrolled, Buddy actually did it, but I helped him. I did whatever I could to prop him up in ways that would let his brilliance come through. In fact, I knew Buddy was a brilliant man and I was fascinated (and a little confused) by how frightened he was at the prospect of going to Harvard. One time after his first three weeks in Boston he said, "I'm in over my head. I can't do the math!" But I told him we had almost a year until he had to go back to Massachusetts, which meant we had to study.

I called Rollins College and enrolled in a night adult education program for Algebra 1 and Algebra 2. Again, I say "we" studied because I already took it in school and had an idea how it should go, which helped us work on it together. I remember late one night sitting at the kitchen table while we struggled with those darn math problems. My fifteen-year-old son walked in and asked what was going on. When we showed him, that little genius picked up the book and solved the problems in no time. Fortunately, Buddy was like a sponge that would do anything to learn. He pushed right through the algebra courses and went on to tough it out in the Harvard program.

When he was up in Boston for three weeks, I'd fly up every weekend to visit. His classmates were fascinating people who were all in the same boat. One weekend, Buddy said: "You know, I'm worried because I can't interpret our financial statements completely. I'm relying on too many outside advisers like bankers or real estate brokers to tell me I can buy this or do that. I need to know for myself where our business stands and where it's going."

Like those algebra classes, Buddy pushed on and learned not only financial statements, but complex spreadsheets as well.

The program was a fabulous experience. We got to know a lot of people, and after the course was over we kept in touch with many of them. In the following years we traveled with a few of them around the country, or abroad to places like Europe or Bermuda. We also made annual alumni trips with the group, just like fraternity or sorority colleagues.

***

The Harvard experience showed me even more of my husband's capabilities. He was kind of a visionary, but I have to admit there were times I doubted him, like when he foresaw the need for a computer program to help the company become more competitive on pricing. He said: "I think we should replace these old *clickety-clackety* things (hand-operated machines) with a computerized estimating program. I looked and there aren't any out there, so I'll make it myself."

That's what he did. Buddy pushed on and it turned out to be the right thing to do at the right time.

He Gave Many, Many People Jobs

I am going to tell you about an ambitious man who started his business in 1958 out of the back of a station wagon at nineteen years old. Helmuth Leo Eidel, also known as Buddy Eidel, was a man who wanted to be in a business for himself. He did not want to work for his dad or for someone else.

He started as a one-man electrician wiring the houses of his friends' parents. For a while, it was only Buddy. When he was able to get a few houses to wire, he did all the wiring and installation by himself. When Buddy started his business, he did not always get paid by the owner. This initially put him in debt. He had to get the jobs, work the jobs, and collect the money all by himself. He had to find ways to eliminate his debt. He accomplished this by being very determined and working eighteen hours a day.

Once Tri-City was up and running, Buddy asked his father, who was also an electrician, to come into the business to help him. It provided both Buddy and his father with a good income. It was a struggle at first, especially since Buddy did not go to college and had no business experience. He had to depend on hiring honest and hardworking employees. One of Buddy's favorite quotes is "When you dance with the gorillas, you have to keep dancing." This means that you can't stop working and you just have to keep going.

Buddy had many accomplishments. One of his best was attending Harvard Business School. Buddy would spend one month a year for three years going up to Harvard. He worked hard or harder during that month than to earn a college degree. He realized that he needed to have business management skills and know about finances so he could make informed decisions.

After forty years of owning Tri-City, establishing a good reputation in Central Florida and adding offices in Fort Myers, Tampa, and Orlando, he was able to sell the company. Buddy knew this was the right decision because he was selling it to his employees. He knew it was in good hands and it would thrive under the new ownership. Tri-City has changed because when the city of Orlando grew, Tri-City grew. Tri-City wired many of the significant buildings in Central Florida such as the Amway Center, and the Dr. Phillips Center.

After Buddy sold the company he did not fully retire. He still worked there day-to-day for three years. Today, he remains on the board of directors. He helps his employees with leadership and knowledge from his experience in the running Tri-City. Buddy considers himself a consultant to the people who now own Tri-City.

Tri-City has changed Buddy's life in many ways. During his career, he met and learned from many great people. It also gave many, many people jobs over the years. Buddy is well known throughout the Central Florida business community for being fair, generous and a man of good character. Anyone who knows Buddy speaks very highly of him.

Buddy is now the subject of a new book. He said he wants people to see how hard work, patience, and perseverance can be so rewarding. He wants people to be able to read about the history and know the story behind Tri-City. He wants to tell people that the harder you work, the luckier you get. He wants people to know the American Dream is alive and well. He also firmly believes in education. All of it requires dedication and a willingness to work hard.

And, most importantly, Buddy is my Grandpa!

By Buddy and Paula's Granddaughter, Jillian Canfield - Age 12

7

Harvard: Buddy's Take

For quite some time I felt like I was flying the business by the seat of my pants. I knew the technical part, the mechanics of the business, but I didn't have the acumen I needed to keep up with our business because we were growing so fast. When I heard about the Harvard program in early 1980, I thought it was a good idea. With Paula's encouragement, we enrolled in the course. The decision came not long after I scared Paula with that $10 million in revenue remark, prompting her to ask me what I was smoking.

I stayed in a dorm with a roommate, and when we weren't in class we all studied in what were called "CAN" groups: about eight people who dissected and tore case studies apart. It was three weeks of non-stop, intense work. The professors came from different disciplines of business, like finance, operations, and marketing. In fact, the program resembled an MBA course in many respects. We also learned a lot from one another during the CAN groups, because everyone came from a relatively successful business and knew a lot about roll-up-the-sleeves issues. After classes and dinner, we got together to preview materials and review the case study for the next day. It was hard work, but overall it was one of best educational experience I've ever had.

When the three August weeks in Boston were over, I wouldn't see any of our classmates until August the following year. That gave me the rest of the year to put some of the principles I learned into our real work environment and brush up on algebra. What was kind of neat was there weren't any other electrical contracting companies in the program. I did have a few general contractor friends from Orlando who took the program at different times, so it was easy to share some of what I learned with them.

After the final third year program, Paula and I kept up with several classmates. One of the more notable people we met in our class was Dean Kamen, an American inventor and scientist whose company invented the Segway, among other technical items. Segways are those two-wheeled people-moving marvels one sees all over parks and museums.

The best part of the program was the insights it gave into the financial part of our business. Knowing that helped get us through some very difficult times with many ups and downs in the economy and industry. We made our share of mistakes along the way, but fortunately we made

THIS IS TO CERTIFY THAT

Helmuth L. Eidel

HAS COMPLETED THE

SMALLER COMPANY
MANAGEMENT PROGRAM

AN EXECUTIVE EDUCATION
PROGRAM OF

HARVARD UNIVERSITY
GRADUATE SCHOOL OF
BUSINESS ADMINISTRATION

GEORGE F. BAKER FOUNDATION

September 3, 1982

FACULTY CHAIRMAN
SMALLER COMPANY MANAGEMENT PROGRAM

DEAN OF THE FACULTY OF
BUSINESS ADMINISTRATION

more good decisions than bad ones, mostly due to the Harvard training. My experience there was so enlightening and inspiring it's still paying off to this day. It was a tremendous amount of work, but I can say I loved every minute of it.

8

New Corporate Digs

The end of the Harvard experience in 1983 marked a major event in my personal life. My mother, Elizabeth Augusta Eidel, passed away in April at the age of seventy-one, just months before my last session. She had suffered from cancer for quite some time and finally succumbed to it. She was such a large part of my life and I miss her to this day. Dad and mom had been married forty-nine years when she died, so a year later we celebrated their fiftieth anniversary anyway by throwing a big party in their honor.

The year 1983 also marked a major change in our business. Tri-City had prospered so much that we outgrew our Maitland facility on Atlantic Drive. Fortunately, a few years earlier I had purchased a 10-acre lot on West Drive in Altamonte Springs with an eye toward moving there eventually. When the time approached, I enlisted my good friend Bill Harkins to help me plan the facility and the grounds. Bill became our general contractor and David Beasley's father, Barney Beasley, was our project manager. The vision was to make it big enough for our current needs with additional space available for expansion.

Completed in 1981, the initial phase only built out half the second floor of the 14,000-square-foot building. Four years later, we completed the second floor with offices for our project managers and estimators. Since then, Tri-City has added several additions to its facility, more recently the Charles J. Eidel Training Building named after my father.

New Home of Tri City – 1981

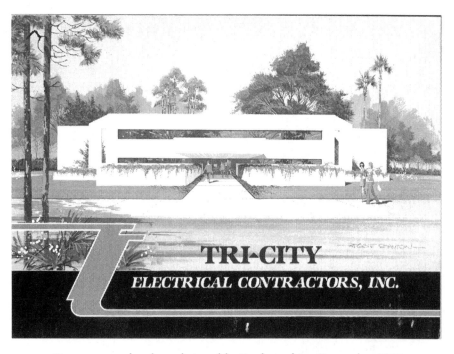

First company brochure designed by Paula and Joe Kawczyk – 1983

My Go-To Contractor

I met Buddy Eidel in the late seventies by default, when Tri-City's offices were located in Casselberry on a little side street. I was only building homes at the time, and Tri-City's Fred Kroker handled the residential end of things. I didn't have any particular impression of Buddy at first, but over time and with more business involvement, our relationship grew.

Buddy is probably the most honest, sincere man I've ever known in the construction business. Because of that, he also attracted the right kind of people to work with him, and they stayed with the company.

Buddy is one of those people who, when he tells you something you can take it to the bank. All the work I did with him in the early days was done without any signed agreements. We just did the work, I paid him, and then we got paid. That was that and it has stayed like that until this day.

It was the same when I built his current office complex, and then his beach house, which is virtually bulletproof. It has deep pilings and reinforced concrete so it's able to stand up against most anything.

Tri-City was my all-around go-to contractor, and that's how it's always been. His firm has done about 90 percent of our work, and it might have had the rest if it had fit our project's mold.

At one time, I had fifty or so people in my company while Buddy had a massive army in his.

Sometimes one of his guys would have trouble with a job, or one of my guys would have problems with their project. When that happened, it never got to an argument: we just called each other, straightened the problem out, and pushed on. Neither he nor I would defend our guy, but we listened to the other and got it solved.

As I mentioned, it's hard to find anyone in the construction business like Buddy where you can look him in the eye and know it will be done. My world is real estate and banking, and his world is electrical and construction, and with such complimentary skills, we came to trust each other deeply. Today, we still get together for lunch and solve the world's problems.

Among other things, Buddy enjoys nice cars. One day after he retired, he bought a maroon top-of-the-line Maserati. Shortly afterward, Rance Borderick, Tri-City's vice president, told me about Buddy's new car. A few weeks later, I was scheduled to meet Buddy for lunch, but I was several minutes late. When I finally arrived, I sat down and apologized for being tardy. I told him, with the straightest face I could muster, that I had gotten tied-up in the parking lot because I smacked into a brand new Maserati. Well, the look on his face was priceless.

Bill Harkins, Founder and Broker Associate: Harkins Commercial

While the new headquarters building was under construction, we expanded our operations into Tampa by opening our first branch office. That was in the fall of 1984. We had grown throughout the Orlando area

Early Eighties in Front of the New Office

and wanted to tap into business opportunities with our major contractors in the Tampa Bay area. Several local contractors wouldn't work with us unless we established an office in their neighborhood.

We bought our office space from Professional Electric, a contractor that went out of business. As I recall we paid somewhere around $300,000 for the facility, which was not pennies on the dollar by any means. I knew the former owners and at one time they were friendly competitors in that area. In fact, they helped us out occasionally when we first entered the Tampa area. Later, when they had projects in Orlando, we helped them by loaning a few of our workers or anything else they needed. Unfortunately, during one of the downturns, they got hit with a few bad jobs and closed.

Professional Electric had a mortgage on the building and hoped to sell it under the most favorable terms, so when we came along it looked like we might be able to help. I paid them what the bank was looking for because I knew somewhere along the way we could have been in the same boat. That's why I didn't try to take financial advantage of them when they were down. As it turned out, it was also a good deal for us because we already had a presence there.

To keep Tampa on an even keel, I adopted the role of branch manager and found myself on the road two or three days a week. But it was imperative to visit the office, job sites, and the general contractors. That kind of hands-on management was important for growing our goodwill, because I didn't know how long it would be until that office made a profit. I really needed a good, permanent manager for the location and the solution would take some time.

Establishing our presence in Tampa set the stage for other Tri-City expansions in Florida. For out-of-town work, we always began with a known general contractor that landed a project and invited us to work with them. Once the foundation was established, and we had gained some credibility with local companies, we worked the numbers to determine if we should open a permanent branch office.

That was the case with Tampa and our other branch offices. Although we had this big business machine in Altamonte Springs, it didn't mean the same thing would happen in another area. It simply was not that easy. Success in a new town depended a great deal on our branch manager, which is the reason we had trouble in Tampa. We would always try to promote somebody from within the company; someone who knew our system, our culture, and our business philosophy. But as hard as we tried, than often didn't work. That's why we brought Jack Olmstead in from the outside.

Although it took almost three years for the Tampa office to finally breakeven, it was still a challenge to remain profitable. Competition was stiff, and even with the best of managers, there were always problems when an office was away from the "corporate mothership." Although we had several opportunities, that was the reason I didn't want to expand out of state. We had plenty of business right here in Florida. The only exception was, and still is, when Rance crossed the state line to work on multi-family construction jobs. He has followed several of our developers and general contractors to other states because they know us, trust us, and invited us to work with them. When we get an out-of-state job, Rance (who has a few out-of-state licenses) usually sends our own team of supervisors to the site and hires locals to do the work. Our team will stay in a hotel until the job is done. When the project is finished, Rance packs up the crew and equipment and heads home to Florida.

The establishment of our Fort Myers and Pompano Beach offices went through the same startup iterations as Tampa. Working in outlying areas meant local general contractors would prefer to work with a company that had a local office. That made all kinds of sense for accountability reasons, because if they had a question or complaint they needed to be able to walk into a local brick-and-mortar office. If we just rolled in to town to do a project and left immediately afterward, they weren't interested. That dynamic was our motivator, and after we checked around and determined there was enough work to sustain a branch office, we put a management team together to run the office. All those factors dictated how and when we opened a remote location.

Nice Guys Finish Last

Buddy and I go way, way back. I first met him in 1986, when we were asked to propose an audit of a community bank in Seminole County. Buddy was one of the organizing directors of that bank, and we found out we were members of the same Interlachen Country Club. Later in the mid-nineties, Buddy decided he wasn't satisfied with his current accounting firm, so we became the auditors for Tri-City.

My wife, Peggy, and I went out frequently with Buddy and Paula and it was always fun. We went to a lot of Interlachen "rubber chicken" events, or fund-raisers for local charities. Paula was usually the live one at dinner since she's no shrinking violet.

At first Buddy struck me as a real gentleman, a kind soul. Over the years, any time his name came up, I'd say: "Buddy Eidel is like Leo Durocher, who once said, 'Nice guys finish last.' Well, Buddy is an exception to that rule!"

A Buddy story that stands out for me is when he was nineteen years old working as an apprentice for the Martin Company. Someone chastised him for working too hard and making others in the union look bad. So, he went home and told his dad he wouldn't work for people like that and decided to start his own business. Tri-City survived and thrived to the point he ultimately had to call his dad to join him.

Most people think Papa was the one who started the business. Well, Buddy never let it be known that it wasn't Papa who founded the business, it was Buddy. I always thought that was pretty cool.

Jerry Hilbrich - Member of the Board, KPMG (Ret.)

9

Keep your Eye on the Fish

Throughout the seventies and into the eighties, Florida had transformed from a sleepy backwater to one of America's super states. By mid-1980, the expansion of NASA, the growth of Disney World, zero state taxes, cheap land, and great weather brought around 1,000 new residents to Florida every day. On a broader scale, the entire American economy was firing on all eight cylinders. Some of the boom was due to President Ronald Reagan's tax cuts, government deregulation, and slashes in social programs. As a result, the runaway inflation of the late seventies dissipated, and the country entered a period of immense prosperity that lasted from 1983 through 1987. During that period, Florida's homebuilding industry continued to blossom and land became an even hotter commodity.

A few people I trusted advised me to take some of the company profits and leverage it through a land purchase. Hal Powers, my agent and friend who found that building for me after my offices burned down, brokered a 40-acre land deal in Longwood that looked very promising to me. A bunch of local investors including Jack Gale, owner of Gale Realty (who Hal Powers worked for), and Jim Gooding (owner of Gooding's

Buddy & Paula – Episcopal Church directory – around 1984

grocery stores), were the principals who owned the property. I checked it very closely and thought it seemed like a solid investment. The land was a raw parcel: the only sign of civilization was a straight railroad track right through the middle.

My brother was the CFO of Tri-City at the time, and we sort of collaborated on the deal because he knew I had a dream about developing land. I'd watched general contractors and developers convert big pieces of acreage into office buildings and warehouses, so I thought I could do the same. It was a speculative buy, but we were so assured of continued appreciation that taking such a risk didn't seem so .... so risky. Based on that, we mortgaged the property to the hilt and bought that land. Not long afterward, the economic bubble burst.

Naturally, when the real estate market took a dive, the construction business followed. Business declined, but our mortgage payments kept rolling in faster and faster. It felt like the lenders wanted payments more than once a month — like three times or more. But that wasn't all. Before we had acquired the land, I had bought a commercial building across the street from our old Atlantic Drive facility in Maitland. And there was also the land I had purchased for our new offices, warehouse, and service buildings, all of which carried a mortgage.

Just when things began to look dire, an investor name Bernie Bennett made us an offer. He wanted to buy almost everything we had, primarily the speculative property. We put our heads together with our lawyers and financial advisors and came up with a price for everything except our future office and warehouse location. It was a fire sale of sorts, but we just about broke even and got out of it. We all heaved a collective sigh of relief when the deal was done. Among other things, I learned a lesson about how my ambition almost got me in serious trouble. The thing damn near took the whole company down.

One of the most important lessons I learned from my Harvard professor, Marty Marshall, was this: "If you are fishing, you should keep your eye on the fish." I can't count the number of times he said that, but it really hit home when we were in the middle of our real estate debacle.

It meant that when doing any kind of business one should stick to their business plan and not lose focus. I was an electrical contractor and that is what I did best. I knew nothing about developing land. I took my eye off the fish.

Paula and I were married when that happened, and it caused both of us a lot of angst. When the ink dried on the sales agreement, we remembered our Harvard experience and kept our eye on the fish from that time forward. I learned to stay within my core competencies instead of venturing into something I didn't know.

***

Until that time, we dealt with the small locally-owned First National Bank of Maitland. We had a great relationship with the folks there and I knew the manager very well. I remember he put his arm around me one day, before the bubble burst, and said, "Buddy, we'll do what we need to take care of you." That was the kind of relationship we had. However, before the economy went south, the bank was acquired by a larger chain, Southeast Bank in Miami.

When we had trouble making the mortgage payments and our balance sheet got pretty thin, we got a little sideways with Southeast Bank. The new owners got in touch with me and diplomatically said I should find another bank to deal with. Translation? The bank wanted its money back, so I found another bank after Mr. Bennett bought our speculative land.

I found a new banker I liked named "Mac" McReynolds. Mac ran the Altamonte Springs Barnett Bank, and Barnett's headquarters were based in Jacksonville, just up the road and still in Florida. I felt reassured by Mac that they'd take care of our business. He said, "You know Buddy, a bank isn't only there to help in the good times. We're here to help in the bad times too." Through the years, Mac and I have become good friends. I also made friends with Pete Cross, Barnett Bank's President. It turned out to be a successful relationship for all concerned. We did many deals the old-fashioned way — on a handshake. Mac even arranged an Industrial Revenue Bond loan for our new facility on West Drive. It was a lot of paperwork, but at the time, commercial mortgage rates hovered around 16 percent. The rate Mac got us through the Industrial Revenue Bond was about 4 percent! That was a tremendous deal and a great help to us.

During that era of economic malaise and banking problems, contracts also slimmed way down. One of the jobs I bid on at the time was the Winter Park Telephone Company headquarters building in Altamonte Springs. It was a dual-purpose building for an office and a site for a large amount of telephone switching equipment. The general contractor we bid was W. A. McCree of Orlando, who did most of the Winter Park Telephone Company construction work. At the time, I felt the telephone construction job was a make or break situation; we needed a good mid-sized project to keep our cash flow in the black. I was determined to be the successful low bidder, and it turned out to be a very good project for us. To call it a cliffhanger would be an understatement. Afterward, we went on to do other jobs for W. A. McCree.

On Certain Meetings

I remember sitting in a construction planning meeting with the owners, architects, engineers other subcontractors, and the general contractor. The owner was having a tough time deciding on construction related equipment, so the general contactor leaned over to an engineer and muttered, "If this guy had three toilets to choose from, he'd crap his pants before he decided which one to use."

In another meeting, a general contractor remarked that the owner drove such a hard bargain

> that when they finally reached a deal, you had to count your fingers after you shook hands.
>
> **Buddy**

10

The Magic Kingdom

Tri-City kept pace with the seemingly endless expansion of the eighties. We increased staff in our two offices, kept a rigorous training schedule for our growing number of apprentice electricians, and smoothed out our estimating and bidding process. Meanwhile, the Disney World giant in our backyard expanded its venue through constructing all manner of buildings, offices, and theme rides. Until the late nineties, all that work was done through unionized contractors. But that started to change in 1988, when Disney gradually opened its bid offers to nonunion shops. Its change of policy came as a result of some very unwise union activity, and the last straw was Walt Disney World Swan and Dolphin Resort project.

It began when Disney awarded some of the work to nonunion subcontractors. When the union found out, members organized and converged on the site with placards and boxes of matches. They went way beyond a normal union picket line protest, turning it into a virtual riot by turning over cars and setting things on fire. In so doing, they literally burned their bridges to many future Disney jobs.

Of course, Disney got fed up, since it rightly believed it could draw from both union and nonunion shops for its projects. But it still needed a regular supply of trained workers regardless of its union status, so it came up with a working agreement. Disney set a wage scale that all employer-subcontractors had to pay its workers. The level was close to the union scale of the time, but without all the fringe benefits. Interestingly, Tri-City, and ABC in general, had already recognized the need to be competitive with the unions, so we gradually raised our wages and increased our benefits accordingly. When Disney made its move to hire nonunion shops, it further leveled the playing field among union and nonunion providers, which proved to be the start of yet another upward trend for us. In 1989, we landed our first Disney jobs.

One of our first three projects with Disney involved the Walt Disney World Casting Center. H. J. High Construction, a nonunion shop owned by Stephen High, was the general contractor. When we finished, we landed a contract for Disney's Studio Backlot Tour followed by other Walt Disney site improvements. All three were completed in 1989 and had a combined contract value of $1.5 million. After proving our mettle through a few smaller jobs at Disney World, we started moving up to the meatier projects.

Incidentally, Steve has become a great friend over the years. We have completed many projects for his company and continue to this day doing work for his son, Robert High, who now heads up the company.

Our largest Disney project came in 1991 for its Yacht Club Resort. It was a 1,000-plus room hotel with two wings covering a little more than half a mile. The electrical contract alone was worth $11.4 million, and the general contractor was Enterprise Building Corporation. It was a unique project in that it was a design/build approach that included electrical engineering services as part of our contract.

With design/build, an owner hires a single entity to perform both design and construction under a single contract. That way the owner has only one point of contact for interactions, which makes it easier for the owner and the contractor. The traditional approach for construction is the appointment of a designer on one hand and the appointment of a contractor on the other. But the design/build approach answers the client's wishes right away. It is easier for the owner, costs less through efficiencies, and smooths out the process through compatible in-house design and application. That's how it worked for us. We hired a local electrical engineer firm owned by Doug Matern to work with us on the project.

We got going by setting up a project office on the site with a couple of doublewide office trailers, and brought in about 100 electricians, apprentices, and helpers. One can imagine the logistics of the project, and the potential headaches. We had plenty of those of course, but it turned out to be a very successful project for Tri-City and Disney. Like McNamara Pontiac, the large Disney contract led the way to a long, successful working relationship with them that lasts to this day. Likewise, Disney has kept its level-playing field strategy for hiring both union and non-union contractors.

***

As 1990 approached, Tri-City continued work at Disney while we launched another big project in downtown Orlando. The Orlando Regional Medical Center, an 808-bed hospital, was one of the largest in the region. I believe it was a good thing the project came along because we'd entered yet another recession. Analysts believe it began with the "Black Monday" stock market crash in 1987. That set off a chain reaction of government policies and restrictions that curbed growth, and led to a severe economic slowdown. As usual, when that happens one of the first industries to take a hit was construction. Although the hospital project grossed $1.1 million, Tri-City still felt the effects suffered by the rest of the country. We quickly went into survival mode.

I had to demote our project manager, Charlie Prendergast, to an on-site electrical superintendent for the hospital project. In turn, I appointed myself as the project manager. I'd always stressed to our employees that they were our greatest asset, and I said that straight from my heart. At the same time though, I tried to get their buy-in to another philosophy, that of sharing in the good times and sharing the sacrifices during the difficult ones. That recession was a good example, I believe. It was a tough time, but we managed our way through it.

On Innovation

I have always been a big advocate of developing systems to make us more efficient. For example, our need for accurate estimating drove me to develop a rudimentary computer program to iron-out the complex estimating process. It was very basic but it worked. Today, we use an advanced, commercially marketed program administered by a software company that keeps us competitive and up to date. But at the time, our basic system did the job until something better came along.

We also innovated with our health program. We were one of the first nonunion shops in Florida to provide health insurance for our employees, as well as a profit-sharing program for the entire company. Those actions proved we didn't need to organize to take care of our most important asset: our employees. Without them, we wouldn't be where we are today.

Buddy

Until that recession, Tri-City never had a formal marketing program. So, I thought it was about time to get something going. I got involved with an organization named TEC (The Executive Committee), made up of executives and owners from several local businesses. TEC was non-competitive so we could all share information without concern. It was through TEC that I met Charlie Stuart.

Charlie became the advisor for our marketing program, and I'll never forget his early advice to us: "It is easier to *become* number one than to *remain* number one." He used the example of a guy on top of a ladder, and another guy climbing up the ladder who constantly tugged at the other guy's pants to knock him out of the way. Charlie said we could decide where we were on the ladder; on top or tugging to get there. His point was, if we were on top we had to work just as hard or harder to stay there.

Later I explained that concept to our employees, saying that once we get to the top we should not believe our own bullshit. We had to keep working at doing better and doing more than was expected if we wanted the business to become a fine-tuned machine. I stressed that it was the only way to maintain our place in the industry. I reiterated it in our 1996 *WattsLine*: "Only by making that extra effort for our customers, suppliers, friends, and associates, can we say at the top of our industry. Personally, I'll do whatever it takes so long as it is legal, fair, and profitable. And then I'll share the rewards with my associates and our employees."

Charlie helped us develop a sound marketing program that trained everyone in the company to think like sales people. We paired our project managers with our general contractor project managers. We did the same with our superintendents, pairing them up with the general contractor's superintendents. We did that right on up the line, even pairing our executives with our general contractor's executives. That way their duties weren't changed, altered, or misaligned, but they were encouraged to have the mindset that everyone at Tri-City was in a sales position. That was another part of the strategy to stay on the top of our game, on top of the ladder, along with continuing to develop more efficient methods and job cost controls.

Ultimately though, it always came down to the individual employee with an established mindset of customer service. In that vein, my column in *WattsLine* became a mantra of sorts: "It's not enough for an employee to come to work each day and fulfill his assignment. Unless we know and care about the customer we're serving, the possibility exists there won't be a future assignment to fulfill. Tri-City does not provide your wages and benefits. Our customer does! Our mission is to do more than is expected. Our customer expects accurate, competitive bids. Our customer expects financial and bonding capability. Our customer expects trained craftsmen. Our customer expects quality installations. Our customer expects timely completion of projects. Our customer expects guaranteed work. Our customer expects convenience and efficiency. Our customer expects courtesy and compliance."

Those were the guidelines then and they haven't changed.

Excel and Serve

I came on board with ABC in November of 1986 as its executive director. Later on, they changed the title to president and CEO, although the duties remain the same. At the time, Buddy served on our board until a year later when he resigned. That meant my experience with Tri-City was not so much with Buddy, but with his organization. Yet the effects of his leadership are written all over his company. He started from nothing and built Tri-City into the powerhouse it is now - one of the leading electrical contractors in Central Florida.

When Buddy started, he wanted to build a nonunion company with a merit shop, or open shop philosophy. But, it was difficult to do in those days because the unions influenced so much, from politicians to licensing and just about every environment contractors worked in. Buddy wanted to choose, retain, and pay his employees fairly based on their own individual merit.

Buddy was attracted to ABC because we believe in the same thing about a merit shop environment. And we also build relationships with politicians and such, so there was a natural attraction. We were a resource for Buddy, and Tri-City was, and is, a resource for us as well.

When Disney World was being developed they used only union contractors. But later Buddy managed to break into that market. He achieved that by offering lower cost and providing above-standard performance. Eventually he got more and more business. But it wasn't only lower prices; it was about doing what was expected, and on schedule. He built his company based on that philosophy.

Then in the eighties, some of the community of contractors decided to get involved in the apprentice program. They incorporated the best parts of what ABC already offered and built their own system of training. Buddy was a big part of that evolution. The contractors went on to develop a spinoff called FEAT, or Florida Electrical Apprenticeship & Training. The result of that effort is that students have gone on to be exemplary leaders of many companies.

One example is Mike Cornelius, a recent ABC chairman. Mike also worked for Tri-City. Mike went through the apprenticeship program where he grew from apprentice, to journeyman, to superintendent, and on up the ladder. He was also a graduate of FEAT and became one of the best chairs we ever had. Mike's story is typical of the kind of people who go through Tri-City's training.

Buddy's philosophy of running that organization was to give people an opportunity to excel. In so doing, he attracted many great people. David Beasley, a Tri-City executive vice-president, was one on them. David served on the board of ABC. Today we also have C. L. Janeski, another Tri-City employee. Since 1986, I can't recall one time when at least one of our members weren't from Tri-City. People like C.L. and Jack Olmstead have continued that tradition.

One of the things we do for our industry is recognize outstanding companies in areas such as excellence in construction. We've done that for twenty-seven years and Tri-City has won those awards in every category every year. The criterion is quite rigid: we have industry professionals, such as architects and engineers, visit various jobs to judge the quality and evaluate the work.

Tri-City has also been recognized for its safety program. When a company in our industry has a good safety record it will attract more people, and better people, which increases its status in the industry.

Mark Wylie, President and CEO, Central Florida Chapter Associated Builders and Contractors, Inc.

11

New Southern Territory

When we started Tri-City, I never thought I'd be doing much work in Miami, which is 235 miles to our south. However, in 1993 business in that area had reached the point where it might have made sense to open a remote office there, like the one we opened in Tampa. As everywhere else, general contractors in Miami wouldn't take us seriously unless we had a tangible presence.

There was another company based in Miami with a startlingly similar name: Tri-City Electric Company, a.k.a. TCE. They established in Miami in 1946, were a union shop, and had a longstanding relationship with NECA, an association of union members. Until then, we worked in the Miami area under our name, Tri-City Electrical Contractors. But when business ramped up, that became a problem. I found out a year after we opened our shop there, on the eve of Thanksgiving in 1994. I received a letter from the son of TCE's owner, Doug Borden. In fact, I knew Doug through our activities with FAEC, the Florida Association of Electrical Contractors. As soon as I got the letter I asked myself if there was some kind of bad vibe about the day before Thanksgiving since I always seemed to get bad news on that day.

Fortunately, before filing our Florida incorporation papers in 1958, our attorney, Jerry Bornstein, searched corporate names and found Tri-City Electric in Miami. At the time, I didn't give it another thought because doing work way down there was the farthest thing from my mind. So, Jerry advised us to incorporate our company as Tri-City Electrical Contractors, the difference being "contractors," to be sure we had a legal differentiation.

After some wrangling, Doug and I worked it out. To avoid any further confusion, we agreed that when Tri-City operated in the Miami and Broward County area, it would use the name South Atlantic Tri-City. The arrangement has kept the peace to this day. Later on, though, and for pure logistical reasons, we moved our Miami area office a few times, from Boynton Beach, to Delray Beach, and then to Pompano Beach. The latest move was to Vero Beach because we focused on multi-family work for the most part in that area.

Like Tampa, we found the South Florida market area challenging, but for slightly different reasons. The hardest part was finding good help because all the qualified workers held jobs with established electrical contractors there. We tried sending experienced people from our

Altamonte office, but few of our employees wanted to work in South Florida. Nevertheless, our balance sheet still tips in the right direction, so we're still there.

Travel Buddies

Buddy and I were members of the newly formed Interlachen Country Club in Winter Park. That was when I worked as a contractor for the U.S. military, building certain explosive devices. That's all I can say about that, except my business and Buddy's were entirely different so there was no overlap. Buddy and I got together around 1986, after our wives played golf and took a liking to each other. They convinced us all to go out to dinner, and after that, Buddy and I played golf frequently.

From the start, I thought Buddy was a real straight up guy who was a lot of fun. He wasn't a braggart, was easy to get to know, and didn't seem to have any faults. His wife, Paula, is very social and also a lot of fun. After all these years, we still spend a lot of time with them. We've taken trips to Italy, Bermuda, and Carmel, California.

Years ago, the four of us were on our way to Bermuda to play some golf. We were on the freeway heading for Tampa to catch a flight, and we thought our golf clubs and bags were secure on the roof of the SUV. Without warning, Buddy's bag slipped its moorings and fell off, only to be immediately run over by the tractor-trailer behind us. When the dust cleared, we gathered as many beat up and bent

---

clubs as we could find, put them in the car, and proceeded to catch our flight.

Buddy didn't get upset at all. In fact, we were sort of glad for him because he had another excuse to buy a new set in Bermuda. He was always happy for a reason to buy a new set of clubs.

Then there was that trip to Italy. Buddy and Paula left for a couple of weeks and didn't expect any visitors, but Janne and I decided to head over there to surprise them. After we arrived, we took a taxi to their hotel and waited below their balcony. It wasn't long before Buddy looked out his window and saw us waving to him from the street. When the shock wore off, we had a great time bumming around the country.

My fondest memories of time spent with Buddy and Paula were on the golf trips to Carmel, California. Over the past seven years, they rented a house for a month or so near Carmel and we'd fly out to spend a week with them. We took in a lot of golf and ate at some of the finest restaurants, including the Mission Ranch Restaurant which was our favorite. We'd eat outside and watch a flock of sheep graze in in a nearby field with a gorgeous view of the bay in the distance. That, and playing the many golf courses in the area, made for many fond memories.

Thurman Kitchin, Retired Government Ordinance Contractor

Thurman Kitchin, Harrison Slaughter, and Buddy at Paula's 60th birthday party –2000

12

Plenty of Work in Florida

Some may wonder why, if we're a very successful contracting company, we don't expand beyond Florida. The answer lies in that credo I learned at the Harvard program: "Keep your eye on the fish." To stick with our core competencies and capabilities, I knew we would do best by staying within the state. It was difficult enough to manage and make a profit with our in-state branch offices. When there was plenty of work here, why extend our reach beyond what we could effectively fulfill? Besides, we had neither the staff nor the interest, and our apprenticeship program and our labor base were here, even though Rance held licenses in several southeastern states.

There was another reason, perhaps the strongest, to stay close to home. My electrical contracting market strategy targeted a niche, a sizeable "in-between" market between two ends of the spectrum that had become very competitive in Florida. I had noticed a kind of divide, a gap between jobs too small for the big contractors and too big for the small ones. The niche lay between two major types of projects: the big-ticket "mega jobs" usually performed by large out-of-state or national contractors with a bonding ability above most in-state contractors, and the smaller jobs handled for the most part by local Florida contractors. That's the strata we pursued, and that's where we grew. After a while, we moved on to the bigger projects that we do today on a regular basis.

Back then, there were many commercial office buildings going up all over town as well as public, state-owned facilities. One example is the Orange County Convention Center, which we bid and landed. Once we completed that, we were really into the big projects. We also wired the original addition and renovations to the Tangerine Bowl in Orlando, another significant project at the time. Those were our "over-a-million-dollar" projects, and bonding a million-dollar job back then was a big deal. Not only did we need to have the financial capability, we were required to have the labor and logistical wherewithal.

On Hiring the Right People

Contrary to the popular practice in much of corporate America, I always tried to see how much I could pay our people for their work, not how little I could get away with. My motivation was practical as well as right, because all the good people had jobs somewhere else. That meant the ones available for a job might not have the credentials or the work ethic to be good employees. By offering good wages, benefits, and an excellent work atmosphere, we managed to keep the good ones we hired long ago.

Buddy

13

The Duck Walk

As our business in the middle niche increased, so did our bonding capacity and the size of our contracts. Among the notable jobs in that era was the National Hurricane Center, managed by our South Florida office. Located on the grounds of Florida International University near Miami, it turned out to be a very interesting, successful project. The structure resembles an upscale battle bunker, and in fact that's what it's called. Built to withstand a Category 5 hurricane, its 12-inch-thick reinforced concrete walls and special design are meant to save lives, reduce property damage, and issue accurate weather forecasts and analyses. The last thing they needed was to have the Hurricane Center blown away in a bad storm.

Another project I'm particularly proud of is the Amway Arena in downtown Orlando, home of the Orlando Magic basketball team. We wired the original arena, named the Amway Center, or the "O-Rena," back in 1989. Twenty years later, we wound up wiring the replacement building, also named the Amway Center. Our budget for the first one came in at $4.1 million, and the contract for the new center, completed in 2010, was $16.4 million.

What is interesting is the original center was on a different site owned by the city, so the old building languished while the new one was being built. They recently tore down the original, which upset a lot people who thought it could have been used for something else, since it was such a beautiful structure. It was only twenty-some years old, and a very useful building. The city argued that modern systems, safety features, communications nuances and such rendered the "old" one obsolete.

The center was another highly successful project for the company. We did a good job for the city, and there were minimal claims when the job was over. In fact, there weren't many claims for either the old arena or the new one. A "claim" means a delay to completion, whether it was our fault or not. It could be due to scheduling challenges, change orders, and so forth. When that happens, we might be there longer than anticipated, which is even more money for labor and lost opportunity for other pending jobs. We may end up having to work overtime, which is never included in the bid.

Historically, electricians are the last ones working on the job after all construction is finished, right up until the place opens. Electricians literally turn on the lights for the tenants. So, a claim usually originates from us against the general contractor or subcontractor that didn't staff the job properly. Even the best bid estimations cannot prevent claims from happening: then, what should have been a successful project could wind up financially unsuccessful.

Another one of our early projects, in 1975, was the University of Florida's School of Horticulture Sciences in Gainesville. We bid the project to Tuttle/White Constructors, and it helped that co-owners Ed

White and Leonard "Mills" Tuttle were friends of mine. Since that was in our earlier years, we weren't able to bond the job, although we had enough capability for the $1 million project. I remember Ed did all he could to make it possible for us, and he eventually came up with a financial arrangement that allowed us to move ahead. We finished it of course, and on time. That was the first of many successful projects with Tuttle/White.

Then there was Marty Belz. Several years after our first Tuttle/White project came the Peabody Hotel in Orlando, not far from the convention center. Marty, the owner, was a very tough cookie to work with. I give him credit because he was very astute, assembled quite a team of project executives, and had the wherewithal to buy whatever he wanted. That included purchasing his own electrical switchgear, which at that point was somewhat unique. Brent Leckey was our estimator for that job, and Don Owens became our project manager under Gilbane Building Company, the general contractor. John Madden was Gilbane's project executive. I recall those names because we had a particularly tough time getting the contract, and they were all involved. But we got it, and we did it. Everyone was very happy when the lights went on.

In fact, Marty got more out of the contract than we bargained for. He and his team thoroughly examined our cost structure during the negotiating phase, examining every detail of our charges for certain items. Like most owners or developers, they always think whatever they're being charged is too much. Since they owned lots of hotels, building the Peabody in Orlando was not their first rodeo, so to speak.

An interesting aside to that project is its sister hotel, the Peabody, in Memphis. That hotel became famous for its "duck march" routine. Every day at 5:00 p.m., the hotel's "duck master" conveyed a half dozen mallard ducks down the elevator to the main lobby. When the doors opened, the ducks made a beeline across a long, red carpet past hundreds of onlookers with flashing cameras to a fountain in the center of the room. They jumped in and swam around a few minutes. Then, as if by some internal guidance system, they hopped out of the fountain. After flapping their wings to dry off, the duck master guided them back to the elevator for a well-deserved rest in their quarters on the roof.

Marty was so inspired by the duck march that he brought the concept to the new hotel.

Sandcastles

My dad and mom divorced when I was three, and I only saw dad on Sundays and holidays while growing up. But my mom would take us to dad and Paula's house on Sunday afternoons for dinner so we could spend time with them.

Well, of course, dad was a hard worker and I remember him in his den working on various projects, doing bids, and so on. Paula would make dinner for us, and my favorite meal was her spaghetti and red sauce. Sometimes she entertained us with stories, and she'd change her voice to match each of the characters.

Even when we went to the beach, dad worked in his home office while Paula took us to play in the sand. Dad came out sometimes, but he was a workaholic and wanted to make Tri-City successful. I worked at Tri-City during my high school summers in the accounting department as a "floater," or substitute receptionist.

For the longest time I was amazed when dad reached up with his hands and cracked his nose. It wasn't until much later that I found out he was only clicking his teeth behind his hand. I thought he was the greatest because he could do that.

One of the traits I took from my parents into adulthood is my dad's work ethic. He never sits around. He always has to be doing something. He never thought anybody should give him a handout. He worked hard, which is why he was so successful. I hope my own children will have that trait as well, because we tend to spoil them. He was also fair and generous to me, and I'd like to think I'm that way with my children.

Dad never shows his anger. Instead, he'll stew over something before he comes out and tells you. But he won't do it in anger: he'll think it over before he sits down in a calm, cool way and tell you what you need to hear.

Growing up, my dad was my hero and my husband says he's a hard act to follow. I think the best thing about dad is how he interacts with my kids. He played with them when they were little, and now he takes them to the ocean and plays with them in the sand. It warms my heart when I see him interacting with my children like that.

Bethany Canfield, Our Daughter (the youngest sibling)

BETHANY

Paula and our daughter Bethany always loved the beach. I'll never forget the time we and the kids were at a friend's beach house, and Bethany wanted to make coquina soup out of the coquina shells we'd gathered. So, Paula cooked up a soup and those shells stunk up the house so bad that no one wanted to eat it.

When she first went to college, Bethany thought her dad wanted her to study business, but she hated it and dropped out. So, Paula convinced her teaching was probably her calling since she regularly babysat for several families throughout her teens. She took Paula's advice and eventually graduated from Rollins College with a teaching degree. She's been happy in that arena ever since.

When Bethany married John, we held a reception at the Interlachen Country Club in Winter Park. It was the biggest bash of all our daughter's receptions, and although Bethany and John were together for several years before marrying, John was a reluctant groom. After the wedding reception though, he remarked, "If I had known it would be this much fun I would have done this a lot sooner."

They have two extremely nice and accomplished teenagers today.

Buddy

14

Other Memorable Projects

It's interesting to consider all the great projects Tri-City was involved with over the years. The Gaylord Palms Resort & Convention Center in 2002 was the company's largest project to date. Originally named Opryland, ESC (the holding company that commissioned its construction), the organization had to submit restructuring plans to creditors due to their heavy debt. That happened when we were in the middle of the job, but as I recall, we came out of it all right.

The Orange County Courthouse project, which was completed in 1997, was one of the first, if not the first, of our large-scale jobs. By then we had established ourselves as capable of million dollar-plus electrical jobs, so the county invited us to bid along with a few other large electrical companies in the area. The general contractor was Morse Diesel International from New York, and we did the job as a joint venture with B&S Diversified, a registered minority electrical contractor. Because it was a publicly funded municipal project, it required a number of minority-owned companies to perform part of the work.

The project involved the 24-story courthouse plus two, six-story administration buildings and basements, which meant a lot of square footage. We put support staff in place for that job and even hired an on-site administrator. We also assigned multiple superintendents to specific work areas, and broke those areas into sections. It was kind of like starting a small company. In my opinion, that was the beginning of moving to the next level with these kinds of projects.

We started by installing a high voltage distribution system of 15,000 volts in a central energy plant. The courthouse was fully hardened with 20,000 pounds of concrete (the standard typically doesn't exceed 12,000 pounds), because of the 1995 Timothy McVeigh bombing of a federal government complex in Oklahoma City. We also equipped the courthouse with a top-notch security system for judges. Once the judges arrived, bulletproof doors slammed shut behind them and they could enter an elevator to their chambers. I guess judges tend to make a few enemies on the job. The cost for the whole thing was around $100 million, and our electrical work came in at $15.7 million.

Another hefty project was for Harris Rosen, owner of Harris Rosen Hotels & Resorts in Orlando. We actually did three hotels for him under the auspices of Welbro Building Corporation. Gary Brown was Welbro's owner and he was another good friend of mine. The job was similar to the Marty Belz project, although I'm not sure Harris would take it as a compliment to be compared with Marty. Harris was, and still is, a very astute businessman who gets involved in all the details, from light fixtures to plumbing, and just about everything else that goes into his projects. He never used financing for his projects: everything was built on a cash basis, which might be another reason he's so successful.

If we wanted to stay in Harris' good graces, we had to read *A Land Remembered* by Patrick D. Smith. He handed out copies of the book in a preconstruction meeting and told us to read it from cover to cover. The book was about Florida's history between 1858 and 1968, and featured the MacIveys, a family that encountered frontier hardships. The MacIveys rose from dirt-poor Florida Crackers to the heights of wealth and standing as real estate tycoons. The setting was in a nature conservatory near Harris' project, Rosen Shingle Creek resort. Today, it's a very large hotel and golf course and he named one of the hotel's restaurants, "A Land Remembered," after the book. Harris befriended the author and they became very good friends.

We completed Shingle Creek in 2006. I believe Harris was, and is, happy with our work, particularly since I told him I loved the book. Shingle Creek came around the time I ended my tenure with the company.

When I look at these projects and countless others, I realize how integrated Tri-City had become with several reliable, credible companies through the years. I already mentioned Jennings & Sons, but there were several other companies in Orlando, such as Williams Development Company. I worked with their father until Bruce and Alan Williams took over the business. We also did a lot of work for Eugene Kelsey. Later, his two sons, Mike and Bob, assumed leadership of the company. Another one is Steve High of the H. J. High Construction. That business more or less fell into Steve's lap when his father passed away unexpectedly. Today, Steve's son, Robert, leads the business. Walker & Company is another one. Lance Walker let his son, Lance, Jr. take over the business.

We've seen a lot of privately-owned father/son companies pass the baton, which is a real advantage in most cases. Unlike corporations where leaders from the outside come in and take over as virtual strangers, when immediate family members assume responsibility, they have the advantage of a continual line of trust and reliability that comes with them.

A Truly Great Brother-In-Law

I first met Robert (Bob) Randolph when Paula were married. Bob was married to Paula's sister, Nancy. Since the beginning of our relationship, Paula and I would go to Nancy and Bob's house in Clearwater every Memorial Day to watch the Indianapolis 500 race on TV. Paula's family is from Indianapolis, and of course, they were all huge fans of the Indie 500. Since their children and ours were about the same age, our families meshed well. We also took many trips with Nan and Bob, including a fantastic Alaskan cruise.

Bob had a successful career with the Jim Walter Corporation as president and CEO of its windows division. I met many of his associates when he invited me on golf trips with the guys, and had a great time talking business on the greens.

Every August, we invited Paula's parents and Nancy and Bob to our beach house to celebrate John's birthday (Paula's dad). We bought fresh steamed lobsters from Publix and ate them out on the deck. We decided to call our get together, "The Waning Days of Summer." One year, Paula had T-shirts made for everyone with this slogan and a lobster printed on the back.

Later in his career, Bob was responsible for relocating the windows division from Miami to Johnson City, Tennessee. It was a huge undertaking, but he managed it quite successfully. Unfortunately, Bob had to take early retirement because of his health. But, he soon grew bored with nothing to do at home, so I asked him to devise a material purchasing system for Tri-City so we could find the best prices from large quantity suppliers. He said yes, and of course we paid him a salary for his efforts.

Nancy told me the job offer was a godsend, but I responded that it was the same for us. He went on to create a very successful system that our company uses to this day.

Unfortunately, Bob passed away several years ago and we miss him dearly. We still see Nancy and his children as often as possible.

Buddy

On Safety

Early on, as the company grew and we hired more employees, issues of safety were not in the forefront of our thinking. However, worker compensation issues eventually took a greater toll on the personal lives of some of our employees, as well as lost man-hours for the company. But it wasn't just a Tri-City problem: It was endemic throughout the country.

Then in 1971, the government established OSHA, the Occupational Safety and Health Administration, which became the Big Kahuna of safety in the national workplace. Along with many other regulations, strict safety guidelines for the construction industry kicked in. That's when we realized we needed a solid, formal safety plan to comply with all the new regulations. OSHA aside, we knew it was the right thing to do.

Although we never had a serious accident among our employees, we wanted to ensure we never would. As a result, we established our own safety department and dad became the overseer. It was a good thing he did, because the new regulations for worker safety just kept pouring in.

According to a recent report in the Monthly Labor Review, a total of 136 amendments to state worker's compensation laws had taken effect since 1980. Among the many changes, general contractors had become liable for all the employees of a subcontractor, which meant Tri-City as well. Further, the definition of an "accident" included preexisting effects of a previous accident, exacerbated by a current job. It all became very complicated, very fast.

Although we already cared deeply about safety for all the right reasons, now it was a bona fide legal issue. That's why I said it was a good thing dad took a keen interest in our safety issues and became our "safety ambassador."

With the help of a few ABC programs already in place, dad started a company-wide safety program starting with our project managers. He worked his way down to superintendents, and then to the electricians. His job included enforcing the new regulations on all our job sites.

We needed to sell the imperative of safety to our foremen and electricians, to let them know we were serious. Well, dad was everyone's friend and the employees who knew him and who called him "Papa," highly respected him. He visited the jobsites, talked with the employees, and patted the electricians on the back for working safely. He also gently corrected them when they didn't follow safety guidelines.

We demonstrated how serious we were by initiating a reward program for employees, because we recognized they were the backbone of the company, and safety was a major concern in our business. We even printed their success stories in our monthly newsletter, WattsLine. We did it in other ways, too, through bonuses, free turkeys at Thanksgiving, Publix gift certificates, T-shirts, drink cups, decals, and so on. We really made a big deal of the safety issue, and dad did a wonderful job promoting the program.

Years later, after dad passed away, the safety director baton passed to Jim Powers, an older, highly respected journeyman who was ready to get out of the field. Today, Mike Powers (Jim's son) is our safety director. He does an excellent job, is very astute with the specifics of the OSHA requirements, and makes sure Tri-City complies with all of its regulations.

> We host an annual banquet at the end of the year and give out awards for longevity, ranging from five to forty-five years. We have always incentivized our employees to work safely. Having said that, I always scratch my head when I think about having to convince them to work safely when all we want is to keep them from getting hurt.
>
> **Buddy**

15

Supplier Appreciation

It was inevitable that Tri-City would purchase ever-larger amounts of supplies for our projects. As such, we became increasingly dependent on the integrity, accuracy, and prompt delivery by our suppliers to meet our needs. In short, we pushed a lot of money in their direction. So, as it goes in the business of buy and sell, our major suppliers of electrical components showed their appreciation by taking a few of us on special trips. One trip came from General Electric Supply, then under the management of Fred Massey. To show his appreciation, Fred sponsored our trips to the Masters Tournament in Augusta, Georgia for several years. While there we made many friends, even with our competitors.

Another supplier sponsored a fishing trip to Cozumel, Mexico. Bob Veazey, our chief estimator, and Jim Hodgkins, from Orange Plumbing in Orlando, and I flew to Mexico City, where we spent our first night in a nice hotel. During cocktail hour and at dinner, I apparently drank too many vodka gimlets and woke up the next morning with half-closed eyelids and a throbbing headache. I don't believe I've had a vodka gimlet since.

The next day, we drove to Cozumel and went fishing on the official yacht of CED, an electrical distributor. We stayed on the boat three nights and fished all day, every day. At the end of each day, the captain and mate teamed up to cook all the mahi-mahi we caught. I have to say those were the most delicious fish I've ever eaten.

Butch Slaughter and Bernie Dempsey were law partners in Orlando, and Tri-City used their services on occasion. Bernie lived around the corner from us in Quail Hollow, and in late August one year Butch and Bernie invited me to go sailing on their boat, Wild Turkey, a 65-foot ketch complete with a captain and a mate. We sailed out of Port Canaveral and headed south to Fort Pierce. Sometimes there wasn't a whole lot of wind during the day, so it got a little boring just sailing around out there. But one day when an afternoon storm popped up, Butch and Bernie encouraged the captain to get some "blue water over the lee rail." So, when a few good gusts blew in, the captain steered into the wind to see just how far he could heel the boat over until blue seawater spilled onto the deck. Well, that scared the hell out of me because it felt like the damned boat was about to capsize. But the captain smiled reassuringly and told me there was no way the boat could turn over. That helped, but not much.

While I was on the boat, Paula accompanied Bernie's wife, Mary, on a private plane to West Palm Beach for a two-day shopping trip. When we got back from our respective trips, Paula told me something had happened to them on the plane. As the plane was leaving Orlando it flew through a torrential rainstorm. It was quite scary, and for several minutes it was kind of iffy. But they survived. That night they went to a restaurant and bar in West Palm Beach for dinner where a couple of octogenarian farmers from Iowa tried to pick them up. Lucky for me she refused. So, I almost lost my wife early on our marriage.

Dinner with the Kids

By the time we closed on the sale of our business we were approaching the new millennium, the twenty-first century. It was also the year of the fortieth birthday of our oldest daughter, Stacia. To celebrate all that, I thought we would take a wonderful family trip. We took a family vote and decided to go to Hawaii for New Year's Eve.

I spent the next five months planning our ten-day trip: first to Honolulu, then the Big Island of Hawaii, and then to Maui. Buddy and I paid for everything, including airfare, room, board, and entertainment. We had a special birthday party for Stacia, spent New Year's Eve at a party at the hotel, visited Pearl Harbor, took boat trips, and played a lot of golf.

Because they were kids, I thought they'd want to spend much of the time on their own and not feel they were joined at the hip with us. So, I told them I'd plan only three family dinners during the trip and the rest of the time they would be on their own. But a funny thing happened: every evening we somehow ended up around the pool, and a sister or a brother would ask the others what they were doing for dinner. Then they'd ask us what we planned. As it turned out, we all ate together as a family *every* evening.

After that, whenever one of the kids turned forty we took another family trip. Since then we've been to places like Bermuda, Cabo San Lucas, and Palmetto Bluff, South Carolina. Each time, we gathered experiences and memories to keep our family together. And most times we wound up eating dinner together.

Paula Eidel

Family in Hawaii for the millennium 1999-2000

16

Prelude to a Debacle

Sometime in 1995, Tri-City received an invitation to join a rather exclusive national group, the Electrical Quality Circle (EQC). Bill Love, owner of SKC Electric, had formed the EQC that year and encouraged us to join. The EQC was a small group of contractors across the U.S. None of the companies competed with the others because each location, or market area, was large enough or far enough away to prevent overlap. The original eight companies were:

- Rivera Electric of Englewood, Colorado
- The Garfield Group of Cincinnati, Ohio
- Consolidated Electrical Group (Bill Love's company) of Lenexa, Kansas,
- SKC Electric, also of Lenexa, Kansas,
- Town & Country Electric of Appleton, Wisconsin
- Wilson Electric Company of Scottsdale, Arizona
- Helix Electric of San Diego, California,
- Tri-City Electrical Contractors of Orlando, Florida

We decided to join the EQC because we wanted to learn from the other companies and share best practices, such as financial statements, business plans, and just about anything else. In short, we thought the group would provide synergy and practical ideas. It turned out to be a very interesting experience for me, and for many in the company, and Bill did an excellent job orchestrating the whole thing. The companies rotated hosting duties from time to time, meeting in respective company offices for a couple of days. Sometimes there was extra time to sneak in a game of golf.

Meanwhile, Bill had been researching the possibility of creating a "roll-up" merger, a popular concept at the time in which investors acquire and merge multiple small companies in the same market. He had contacted a construction consulting group, FMI, or Fails Management Inc., run by Doc Fails, an executive in Tampa who could analyze the potential value of our EQC companies as a group. Rollie Stephenson, of Town & Country Electric, had in-house expertise on how to form roll-ups based on his experience with a friend whose company had been rolled-up by a Wall Street operative, Jonathan Ledecky. Based in Washington, D.C., Jonathan had raised a lot of money to roll-up the fractured service businesses. He was interested in buying only well-established companies, not fixer-uppers.

One of Rollie Stephenson's friends, Dan Spaulding, who was president of School Specialty, was in the office supply business when Ledecky had been acquiring fragmented mom-and-pop office supply companies into one big conglomerate. Dan joined, and he seemed to be profiting from the arrangement. Apparently, Ledecky raised another $500 million to do the same with electrical contracting companies.

While this was going on, Paula and I had approached retirement age and had begun looking for an exit strategy. But we didn't see any way out of our continuing dance with the gorilla. We would have loved to sell the company to the employees, but we had grown so large, we didn't think the employees could buy the company and handle the debt service. If we sold the company and relinquished our day-to-day control, we didn't want to be on any personal bank or bonding financial guarantees. In a way, we had become victims of our own success because even if they were very profitable, the jobs kept getting bigger, riskier, and more litigious. We were at the point in our lives that we wanted to smell the roses before it was too late.

Paula, more so than me, was ready to sell the company. After much discussion, we sought the advice of my good friend and CPA, Jerry Hilbrich, a trusted advisor and confidant. Jerry had advised us against a previous buyout offer by pointing out the various pitfalls. We were glad we turned that one down because the Ledecky proposal looked so much better. Based on much thought, introspection, and Jerry's advice, we decided to look into it.

Ledecky's idea was to consolidate similar electrical contractors within a geographical area and their sales, marketing, service, and other units, into one large company. With "strength in numbers," and economies of scale, the roll-up could theoretically forge a powerful front against the competition, gain stronger buying power, and provide financial clout.

They presented their idea to us and we thoroughly investigated the prospect. According to Ledecky, he would incorporate all of our companies into one big company, but Tri-City would still remain autonomous. The only thing he asked for was a commitment to stay on board and not run out after we got paid. If we moved forward with it, the decision would involve investment bankers, consultation with our local bank, other financial advisors, and a financial company named Mid Atlantic that advised us along our path. It was an intriguing idea, but was it for us?

17

Is it Time?

Paula and I thought long and hard about how we could retire from the business. We longed to be relived of the responsibilities of personal bank guarantees for numerous lines of credit, and contractor surety bonding lines. I'd already passed sixty years of age and we were getting to the point where we wanted to take a long break to smell the roses. My decision to sell the company was further complicated by another factor: Considering the way I was built, I was either in the business 100 percent and controlled all of it, or I was completely out. If I could not control it, I didn't relish the idea of a huge, continuing financial responsibility hanging over my head. As they say, "You're never half pregnant … you're either pregnant or you're not."

The thought of retirement was also bittersweet. I loved the business and our employees. Saying goodbye to them would be the hardest part, harder than telling them I intended to sell the company.

There were compelling reasons to sell Tri-City to Ledecky. During our negotiations, Ledecky assured us he would not change our company management. He also said he would leave us alone because we were all doing well, which was the strongest reason he wanted to buy the company in the first place. Furthermore, all the owners and presidents of the companies had to agree to stay on for five years to ensure we couldn't "fire sale" the Building One stock we acquired when we sold the company. To be sure, there was a "lockup period" on our stock, meaning it could not be sold for a certain length of time.

Following a lot of critical thinking and the advice of many counselors — particularly our CEO, Chuck McFarland — we sold our company to Ledecky. We're not just talking about Tri-City and all the EQC members: after he bought our entire group he kept right on going. While all that was going on, I had to remember when he said, "Just keep on doing what you've been doing, and I'll support you and take care of you."

Initially, his company was named Consolidation Capital. Not long after, and to better identify the group, he changed it to Building One Services. Later, the name changed again to Encompass. Here are excerpts from an article that came out after we agreed to join Ledecky's group.

U.S. Chain Buying Tri-City Electrical

The Altamonte Springs Company Is One Of Seven Electrical Contractors Being Acquired By Consolidation Capital.

January 31, 1998|By Suzy Hagstrom and Jack Snyder of the Orlando Sentinel Staff

An old, well-known electrical contractor in Altamonte Springs announced Friday that it will become part of a national chain. Tri-City Electrical Contractors Inc. is one of seven contractors being acquired by Consolidation Capital Corp. of Washington, D.C.

Tri-City's president, Helmuth Leo "Buddy'" Eidel, said the acquisition would not change the company's operations or management. Eidel, 59, said he would sign a five-year employment contract to serve as Tri-City's chief executive officer.

Eidel would not say how much Consolidation Capital is paying for Tri-City. However, the deal to buy all seven electrical contractors is valued at $138 million in cash and stock, with half of that in stock. The transaction is expected to close in February.

Consolidation Capital, which went public in November, is led by Jonathan J. Ledecky, who started U.S. Office Products Co. by buying mom-and-pop office supply stores throughout the country. Eidel founded Tri-City as a family business in 1958.

"At this stage of my life and career, this is the best thing, not only for myself but also for my employees," Eidel said of the acquisition. Being part of a larger company will give Tri-City better employee benefits, greater buying power, improved training and more resources, he said.

The idea of joining a national chain of electrical contractors grew from a peer group that Eidel has participated in during the past three years. The group, called Electrical Quality Circle, is a forum for sharing ideas and discussing problems. Some of its members also agreed to join Consolidation Capital.

A Shiny Kind of Guy

It was wonderful growing up with Buddy and Paula Eidel. They were always supportive and were always there for me. Buddy filled the void and was a great father.

I was married in Orlando in the Emmanuel Episcopalian Church, and both Buddy and my biological father walked me down the aisle. I always loved my biological dad, but I have to say I loved Buddy slightly more because my biological dad was not an integral part of my life.

When I was growing up, Buddy had funny nicknames for all my boyfriends. The top three name were: "Meathead," because this one wasn't very bright; "Captain Marvel," because he wore a huge, orange helmet; and "The Italian Stallion," because he was, well, very Italian with a thick accent from New York. The Italian Stallion had me over for spaghetti dinner with his family one time, and they called the sauce "gravy" even though it wasn't gravy ... it was spaghetti sauce. The only one he didn't have a nickname for was my husband, Clark, because he and Mom really liked him and thought he was a normal person.

I was very rebellious in high school, so they called me the "Viet Cong in tennis shoes," because the Viet Nam War was going on at the time. Still, they kind of sloughed off my shenanigans because I didn't get into any big trouble.

I didn't appreciate it at the time, but they occasionally had one of their surprise weekends. They did it once every few months and called it the "family mulch day." They had mulch delivered to our driveway, and intentionally had it dumped in front of the cars so we couldn't get out until the mulching was done. We tried to sleep in, but that didn't' work. The mulch would stay there until we took care of it. It took most of the day to get it done, so we did it as fast as we could.

My parents taught me to treat people the way I wanted to be treated. Mom and dad were always very fair and loyal, and made me very thankful for what I had. I also learned that hard work definitely paid off in the end. I worked hard in school and after school, but I could never work as hard as Buddy. He thought nothing of going in to work at 4:30 in the morning and going all day.

They disciplined us, but with a gentle hand. If I came home past curfew, I would just say, "Okay, I'm grounded, right?" They'd answer, "Yes." But it wasn't anything horrendous, just enough to make me think twice the next time.

Compared with my other friends' parents, I'd say Buddy and mom were the kindest, most loving parents ever, and they still are. They're great with my kids, particularly my son.

One of the nicest things my mom says about Buddy is that he is, "One of the shiniest people I know."

Dr. Stacia Goldey – Our Daughter

STACIA

Stacia, our oldest, was a scholar and also very active in school as a cheerleader and editor of the high school yearbook. She was continually in a hurry. Her first car, a red Nissan two-door tin can, rattled the neighbors as much as the vehicle. They often complained when she'd peel around the corner and come screeching to a halt in our driveway. Her hair curlers were strewn over the car floor as she went racing out to school in the morning, combing her hair as she drove. When she graduated high school, we bought her a tiny bronze colored Plymouth with a stick shift. Even though she had never driven a stick before, she drove it home from the car lot. Quite a sight!

She graduated Summa Cum Laude from the University of Central Florida and went on to graduate second in her medical school class at the University of Florida. Naturally, we are very proud. When Stacia got married to Clark, she arranged for both her father and I to walk her down the aisle. That was a fine moment in my life.

Buddy

18

Temporary Relief

It was a bittersweet decision to sell the company. But after many, many years of nonstop involvement in the business, we knew it was time to take a different path. To be honest, I hadn't lost my enthusiasm for the business, which might be the case for others in my position, but it was time to give our management and employees an opportunity to grow, and maybe become part owners in the company.

I hired Jack Olmstead on April 3, 1995, when we had problems with profitability and management at our Tampa branch office. From the onset, Jack and I were joined at the hip in many ways. I brought him up to speed with the Tampa office and Tri-City's procedures and methods as soon as I could. In fact, I hired Jack with the thought in mind that he might someday become president of the company. David Beasley also could have filled that role. At the time, the bank and our bonding company were leaning on me pretty hard to establish a solid succession plan for the company. However, David was very close to my age, so they felt he wasn't the right fit for our succession plan. I sensed the need for new blood and fresh ideas to prevent the company from growing stagnant. So, when the time came to transfer the company to Building One Services, I knew my role would change and I should continue grooming Jack for the presidency.

Eventually, Jack was appointed president of Tri-City. Jack was a perfect fit for the job, and management was completely in favor of him assuming the role. Once he took over, I trimmed my daily office visits back significantly to get out of his way and let him run the show. I did not want him to feel like he had to work in my shadow.

Jumping forward a bit, I must say that Jack has done a fabulous job. He has weathered an economic downturn, and kept things going when a couple of key shareholders left the company. That put us in a real financial hardship, but Jack, along with the rest of the management team, navigated those very difficult times. Add to that the untimely passing of Chuck McFarland: Jack and the management team turned right around and replaced Chuck with an excellent CFO in the person of Mike Germana, who fits the Tri-City team like a glove. Since Mike joined the company, his department has never skipped a financial beat.

Tampa Office

***

Admittedly, I enjoyed being involved with the company while we were under Building One and Ledecky, but the management team in Houston had changed considerably. It seemed like they were far more concerned with the numbers than with the company.

Keep Buying!

To rewind again, …

After we were sold to Building One, we kept right on doing what we'd been doing since 1958. True to his word, Ledecky didn't interfere. It stayed that way for about a year before Wall Street became restless. The investors didn't think Ledecky was using their $500 million the way he should; they expected a swifter return on their investment than they got. When I say Wall Street, I'm referring to the investors who bought equity (stock) in the merged companies. Essentially, the investors were the ones who owned Ledecky and the rest of the business in the group. What contributed to their anxiety early on was the perception that we were all hard dollar contractors who performed some aftermarket service as well as construction work. To make the company more appealing to Wall Street, and address the anxiety, Encompass, which acquired Building One, applied pressure on its companies to gain more service business. It turned out to be an excellent decision. To this day, our company performs a lot of service work as a result.

Wall Street was always hungry. They wanted more and more growth in revenues and profit, which drove Ledecky and the others at the top to merge our companies with another group, an HVAC (heating, ventilation, and air conditioning) roll-up called Group Mac. The premise was that Wall Street would view positive synergy in the combination of an electrical contractor group and an HVAC group, because like us, Group Mac had some very good companies. It turned out to be false hope, and led the organization on a buying spree, which turned out to be fatal in the long run. In the meantime, Group Mac's corporate headquarters relocated to

Houston and Joe Ivey, of Ivey Mechanical, assumed the role of CEO. That's when they changed the name to Encompass. Interestingly, our stock price didn't appreciate the move as much as we thought it would. In the end, the only thing Encompass encompassed was two different disciplines and a huge corporate staff in Houston desperately trying to manage the unwieldy organization it had become.

Corporate tried to satisfy Wall Street with projections, profit numbers, and such, but that didn't work so well. They went on to buy more and more companies to shore up the flagging margins. Ultimately, it became a bad experience. Corporate bought companies that proved to fall below the quality that had been presented, and that added to the financial problems. Within five years, the whole roll-up thing went bankrupt.

When this book was about to go to print, I happened to be reading a copy of *Barron's Weekly* financial magazine and came across a quote by Warren Buffett. He said, "When companies (are) living by so-called making the numbers, they do a lot of things that are really counter to the long-term interests of the business." Buffet's words struck me in a profound way because twenty years ago I heard essentially the same thing from someone else. At the time, Charlie Walker of Walker Engineering in Dallas (one of the new Group Mac companies), said, "If we keep playing to Wall Street, this whole thing is doomed." How farsighted Charlie was at the time. As they say, "The rest is history."

We came full circle. Jack, with Chuck McFarland (by far the most astute CFO of our entire group), and Tri-City management purchased the company out of bankruptcy from the court in Houston for pennies on the dollar. A lot of money went down the drain. In the process, I also lost a considerable amount of money because I held on to my Encompass stock way too long. By that time, I'd been away from the company and fully retired with Paula.

The Tinkerer

Buddy was always tinkering with stuff. He'd tinker with spreadsheets and arrive at the office the next day with something new. He was always very receptive of people with new ideas, and was always checking things out to find a better way to do something. That's why we called him the Swiss Watchmaker. Chuck McFarland came up with that name because Buddy had every little thing under his magnifying glass. Well, Buddy is German and he kind of looks like a watchmaker anyway.

He loved to talk about how to do something better. Some days he'd arrive early with a brand-new model of something he construed in his mind.

But you know, he's an amazing person. In the entire history of Tri-City he never walked away from anything. He never paid one dollar of delay charges or fines for a job for not being done. In fact, we have never not finished anything. It's almost a fault sometimes because clients know Tri-City will finish the job no matter what, whether we're making money or not.

Buddy was also a very good listener. In meetings he'd listen, but in due time he would show his own side of the situation. And when he had enough, he'd had enough. He'd practically jump up on a table and say, "Okay, I listened to you and now you're going to listen to me." Whether it was an unruly customer, vendor, or an employee, after listening he'd give his opinion.

Buddy also had a fuse that was long and patient. But if burned for too long, he'd finally pop. I think that's the German in him.

He surprised me a couple times when I first joined the company, because he was always so quiet and soft-spoken. One time a couple of guys had done something and I happened to be in the meeting. After a while, they made like Michael Jackson doing the moonwalk to back away from Buddy's desk. He was that hot. I can honestly say it was good to see him get that way every so often because he had to make it right: he had to set the record straight.

He always had quotes to fit the need of the moment. In meetings he might say something like, "Don't check your brains at the door," or, "Work on the business, not just in the business" and, "The harder you work, the luckier you get." I should have been writing all these down all these years, because they were zingers.

I can't say enough good about Buddy. He and I hit it off early, and it's worked out very well for me. I believed in him and would follow him anywhere.

Jack Olmstead, President of Tri-City Electrical Contractors

19

New Beach Digs

Not long after we closed on the sale of the company, I started plans for our house in New Smyrna Beach. We'd purchased an empty lot right on the ocean several years earlier, and it took another eighteen months to get the plans and permits before we could start construction. Bill Harkins was my general contractor, and I enjoyed working with him and Bill's son, Matt, who was the project manager. It took another year to complete the house, and we finally moved in on the July Fourth weekend of 2002. Our family has enjoyed that house very much, particularly when our grandchildren were younger.

Soon after completing the beach house, Sam Ewing and Gail Winn, of Ewing Noble & Winn, began redecorating our Alabama Drive residence. Sam showed us plans for a spec house that he and Gail had developed. Located on Greentree Drive, on Lake Osceola in Winter Park, it was very close to our Alabama Drive home. I was quite enamored with the plans because it was on a lake, and I'd always wanted a house on the water. It also had an office/library. Our interest grew, and one thing led to another. We made a deal with Sam and Gail to buy that lot and the house plans and hire them as our interior designers when it was ready. It took about two years from start to finish. In March 2007 we moved into our beautiful new home. Paula and I have enjoyed it and have many fond memories with our family and friends there.

After building the Greentree Drive home, I was ready to slow down a bit more and settle into retirement. As my good friend Pete Cross used to say when people asked him how he liked retirement, "I am so busy being retired I don't know how I had time to work." I subscribed to Pete's saying because I have never regretted retiring. Not one bit. I believe the key to successful retirement is to keep busy doing what you enjoy and doing it on your own schedule.

I have remained connected to Tri-City since I've been allowed on the board of directors and attend the monthly financial and staff meetings. I also continued to serve on the board of the Orlando Philharmonic Association for a couple of years. I also like to work with our financial advisers team at Goldman Sachs' Dallas office, where I perform monthly reviews and our two financial advisors visit at least once a quarter. In response, their office has helped us with our personal portfolio, and how to weather the ups and downs of the financial markets.

I am currently involved with remodeling a new condominium we purchased at The Residences in Winter Park. Once again, Sam Ewing and Gail Winn are our interior designers. We hope to move in by September of 2018.

As if we didn't have enough to do already, Paula and I manage to travel with the Electrical Quality Circle owners, and with friends made during my Harvard years. I play a little more golf now and then … about four days a week with buddies and with Paula. Paula and I enjoy many Sunday afternoons at the Interlachen Country Club with several other couples. And like all grandparents, we thoroughly enjoy watching our grandchildren grow, complete high school, and go on to college. As of this writing, I still find myself very busy and have no lack of things to do.

My advice to anyone considering retirement is to look at the prospect as positively as you can. After all, it is only another chapter of your life and not the end of it. I urge you to do as many things on your bucket list as soon as you can, because we're not young forever. As my dad used to say, "We work hard and we play hard." You've worked hard, so now is the time to play. So, smell the roses and enjoy life.

Buddy's Blueprint for Success

√ Create a good foundation.

√ Be as efficient as possible, employing good systems and practices.

√ Work smarter, not harder.

√ Do more than expected. Surprise and delight the customer.

√ Never add cost to profit to make up for our own inefficiencies.

√ Treat customers like you want to be treated.

√ Be better than others in the marketplace.

√ Be equipped for the job at hand: proper tools, good facility, and serviced vehicles.

√ Develop a culture where employees respect one another to create an atmosphere of loyalty and dedication. Promote from within whenever possible.

√ Work on the business, not just in the business.

√ There are no substitutes for preparation and hard work.

√ The harder you work, the luckier you get.

√ Don't check your brains at the door.

Buddy at 70th birthday party

III
PERSPECTIVES

Mike Powers

1

From Krystal Burgers to Tri-City

Before I came to Tri-City, I was the assistant manager of a Krystal Burger chain restaurant. That was my first job in high school, and when I got out, I became an assistant manager of the Krystal's next to the Jai Alai court in Orlando. I always worked a bunch of hours, but when I became sick with mononucleosis my doctor wrote a note saying I should only work a 40-hour week for the next two weeks. When my regional manager read it, he cussed me out and said *he* would decide how many hours I should work. I wrote a heated letter to the owner of the company and turned in my resignation the next day.

While I was sick, mom told me my dad wanted me to go into the trade he was in, as an electrician with Tri-City Electrical Contractors. That was forty-five years ago, in 1973, and we were in the middle of a major recession brought on by the OPEC cartel, which sets the price of oil on the world market. Tri-City had to lay off 27 people then, but I took dad's advice and applied anyway. Amazingly, they still hired me. I was a green helper of course, but there was always room for a minimum wage worker regardless of the economy. Years later I took the apprenticeship program to become an electrician, and later on I became a superintendent. That was quite a journey from flipping burgers.

Right after I became an electrician, Tri-City was involved with a job at Valencia College East Campus. We were wiring a new three-story classroom and auditorium when a special project came up. That was when Buddy served as project manager for certain jobs, as well as the CEO of the company. My dad was on that job and they placed me out there to help. One day Buddy, my dad, and a few other electricians gathered in the electric room to observe a new fastening product, a concrete anchor called Tapcon. The sales rep was there making his pitch.

This product was supposed to solve the problem of attaching electrical wiring to concrete with a light duty fastener. Tapcons had special threads that tapped into predrilled holes in material like concrete, block, and brick. We watched the rep use a big, cumbersome drill, like a hammer drill, to make holes for the Tapcons. When he finished, he turned to Buddy and said: "So if you buy 5,000 of these screws, we'll give you this drill for free." Then he thanked him and went on his way.

Buddy turned to us and said, "Well, dammit Bill and Jim. I had hopes, but I think this is just too expensive."

Tapcons were state-of-the-art, but they cost way too much and the drill was huge. For each electrician to use the Tapcons effectively, they'd all need a drill, which would be even more expensive. So, Buddy, Jim, and Bill found a way to hang wiring from concrete at a fraction of the cost. Their method served us well until the Tapcon fasteners came down in price, and their drills, too.

What I saw in Buddy that day was guidance, wise guidance by finding a way to do the job with far less money. Buddy's thinking was always outside the box, and that kind of thinking is what helps us make money. Those fasteners, along with many other things he studied, made all the difference in the world. It was Buddy's involvement in the details and being a true hands-on guy, even if he did own the company. That made all the difference.

Mom & Dad at a party – 1984

***

My dad was one of Tri-City's top two superintendents when I was hired. Several years later, he was promoted to safety director after Papa Eidel left the position. Papa did a great job, but he was at the end of his career. When dad retired, I applied for the job and eventually got it. That was in 1996.

2

Don't Dispose of Them

Since I was originally hired as a helper, I didn't really get to know Buddy until later. But I had heard a lot about him. I knew he was driven and had goals he wanted to reach. I also knew he was very committed and always looked for better ways to do things. It wasn't that his goal was to reach a certain x-number of dollars over so many years, but he wanted a certain x-number of employees, and that's the goal he pushed for.

In my opinion, there was no earthly reason for Buddy to take that Harvard Business class because he was already very well off. He had all the money he needed and led a company that was well respected and honored. So why did he go? The answer is he wanted to be better. He felt that he was the one holding the company back from moving forward, and so he knew he had to do better.

Tri-City is successful because of its people. If someone underperformed or did something wrong, Buddy, along with Jack Olmstead, didn't just dispose of them. Nobody is perfect, but everyone has value when they use their strengths. Everybody has weaknesses, too, but there was never an attitude of "this guy is less than perfect, so let's get rid of him." Instead, they found ways to encourage people to produce, or to bring out the best in them by placing them in a different position.

One example involves an estimator who screwed up badly. I mean it was a big time screw up. It was the late eighties and he somehow decided a factory we were going to work on had an 8-foot ceiling and planned accordingly. He ran all the pipes up to 8 feet, and ran them all across the factory ceiling and back down. Well, that factory had a 32-foot ceiling, not 8 foot. The job was bid, and when we got to work you can imagine what kind of cost overruns we had. At the time, it was the worst experience of its kind at Tri-City. I was a superintendent back then and I remember making fun of the blunder in the field.

The rest of the story goes like this: that estimator didn't get fired. Of course, he was torn up about the mistake since it cost the company somewhere around $1.5 million. But the estimator didn't get fired because Buddy and the other people at the top believed he would learn from his mistake. That says a lot about the kind of leadership Tri-City has. If people make mistakes, you don't dispose of them, you work with them to make sure they won't do it again.

Sowing Into the Future

I was born on Christmas Eve of 1963 at Winter Park Memorial Hospital. While that was happening, my dad was out trying to buy a coal car for the family train set. That was an important memory because my grandfather gave my dad an entire set and they both assembled it every Christmas Eve. Dad has good memories of that train, and he couldn't bear to throw it away, so he gave it to me. I took it to the model train center in Orlando to learn more about it, since I wasn't so sure how it was supposed to work. I got the answers, and today my husband and I do the same thing around Christmastime.

I have fond memories of growing up with dad. As a senior in high school, I worked half-days at Tri-City and went to school the other half. I also did an internship at the company, and dad set me up in his office and taught me project scheduling, Lotus, and other skills.

Later, at the West Drive office, they asked me to be the receptionist, but I told dad I wanted to work in the accounting department instead. He said it wasn't a good time: that I should wait until the software system was upgraded. Once that happened, I started to learn the billing, inventory, payroll, and basic accounting practices. I thought I would study business in college and wanted to get an accounting degree. The fact that dad let me work in that department had a lot to do with my future.

Dad taught me hard work, tenacity, and persistence. So, I took all that with me when I went to work at Sawtek. Those lessons helped me move up the ladder to the position of controller, when I had seven people working under me. That was significant because those were the days when most positions were occupied by men. That's how dad prepared me to enter a male-dominated workplace and to succeed.

I marvel at how kind and respectful he is toward other people. Even when I knew he'd been embroiled in a dispute with someone else, he still treated them with the same respect he gave everyone. Once he got away from that person, I knew he blew off steam about what they did, but never in front of anyone. I was so impressed. Whenever I meet people who know who I am, and know who dad is, they never have an unkind thing to say about him.

Dad and Paula did a great job when it came to holiday vacations. Paula likes to throw parties and always invites the entire family to places like Hawaii or Montana.

In short, Paula, dad, and all the siblings played well together. Seeing that has affected my life to this day because it was a good example of how to live.

Tammy Collins – Our Daughter

TAMMY

Whenever Paula and I took the kids for ice cream or dessert after dinning out, Tammy would always want a hamburger or French fries instead of a dessert. I couldn't figure that one out, since she had just finished a big dinner at the restaurant. Like her sister, she was always good in school, and also was a great volleyball player. Paula used to make all her uniforms.

Tammy was a hard sell when it came to boyfriends. She would always tell us, "No kids. No pets. No husband. No problems." Well, she went on to marry Reed, the man of her dreams. We had their rehearsal dinner at our home on Alabama Drive, and that evening the weather turned out to be the Storm of the Century. We were all set up with outside tables for dinner, but had to quickly move everything inside. It rained and hailed all night.

Buddy

3

NCCER

When the National Center for Construction Education and Research (NCCER) formed in 1966, several large companies became involved along with about one hundred twenty-five construction company CEOs. There was the Fluor Corporation, Daniels, Halliburton, and Tri-City. As the group put it, we united for the purpose of "Revolutionizing training for the construction industry. Sharing the common goal of developing a safe and productive workforce."

These companies helped fund the center as an original spinoff from ABC. Today, NCCER is affiliated with the University of Florida's M.E. Rinker, Sr. School of Construction Management. The electrical apprenticeship program is now a stand-alone curriculum. Buddy donated $50,000 to NCCER and went on to add fifteen cents an hour from our employee wages toward the program. That meant for every hour worked, Tri-City donated thirteen cents to Tri-City's training program, and the remaining two cents went into the NCCER fund. The NCCER building is in Alachua, Florida, and Tri-City wired the building.

I've been on their National Safety Committee for quite a while and was also "on loan" as a subject matter expert for textbooks. Buddy has always stressed that we all need to give back to the industry, so over the last twenty-three years I've been writing textbook articles for NCCER as well as our company.

Buddy also helped start FEAT, the Florida Electrical Apprenticeship Training program. Today, FEAT is the largest training program of its type in Florida serving around seventy electrical contractors. And here's the kicker: Although Tri-City is a contributor and a recipient of its training for our employees, Tri-City management doesn't choose who goes to school. It's the employee who makes that decision. Most companies tell their employees when they'll go to apprenticeship training and where, using it as a kind of reward. At Tri-City, if an employee has been on

Certificate of Recognition

National Center for Construction Education and Research

Be it known that

Tri-City Electrical Contractors, Inc.

*having met all the requirements of the standardized safety training process
as set forth by the National Center for Construction Education and Research
is hereby declared a*

QUALITY SAFETY PROVIDER

*In witness whereof, over the seal of the National Center for Construction Education and Research,
we set our hand hereunto on this ___13th___ day of ___June___ in the year ___2000___.*

Daniel J. Bennet
President

board ninety days or more they can attend apprenticeship school if they want to. Nobody tells them to go and it's their own decision. That's huge since the decision to train indicates a person's motivation and what's in their heart. If an employee is motivated like that, then the employee will become a strong worker. That philosophy has led Tri-City to dominate the apprenticeship program. As long as I've been involved in training, I've always attended graduation and we're always at the top in terms of the number of graduates.

Incidentally, in 2004, we received ABC's national excellence in construction award for the Ritz-Carlton Orlando, Grande Lakes. And in 2008, Tri-City was designated the "Number One Best Place to Work in Orlando" by the *Orlando Business Journal.*

One of the Pillars

I have been with ABC for eleven years, but I'm kind of a lifer since I took over from my dad, who was there almost thirty years. That means my family has forty-one years of history with Buddy Eidel and Tri-City Electrical Contractors. As a second generation with ABC, I knew about Tri-City long before I knew Buddy. In fact, I met him only once or twice because he was about to retire from the company when I got involved. I know Jack Olmstead more since he became Tri-City's president in 2001. Regardless, Buddy is a legend in our industry, having created Tri-City in his garage and built it into one of the state's top electrical contracting firms.

From our perspective, Tri-City has been an integral part of our membership for almost our entire existence (about fifty years) on the Gulf Coast. It wasn't one of our founding members, since they were based in Orlando when we started, but they've expanded their operations to our area.

Tri-City is recognized by our association and the industry through countless awards for workmanship, safety, and development initiatives. And Tri-City has always had a commitment to training. From our chapter's perspective, no one has trained more electricians through ABC than they have, to become our largest apprenticeship-training sponsor for the last twenty years. That means they have placed a large number of electricians in our program, and the industry.

Starting with Buddy Eidel, and then Jack Olmstead who learned a lot from Buddy, Tri-City has been one of the pillars of our association for as long as I've been here. As long as we fight for the principals of merit shop contactors, I know they'll remain one of our most influential members.

**Steve Cona III, President and CEO
Associated Builders and Contractors,
Florida Gulf Coast Chapter**

Rance Borderick

1

Right out of High School

With the exception of three months working as a laborer, this is the only job I've ever had. After I graduated from high school in 1972, I went to work for a construction company as a laborer doing menial work. I knew I needed to do something else to get launched, and Tri-City happened to be doing the electrical work on that job. While I worked, I kept an eye on them and eventually got to know the superintendent. A few months later, I told him I was interested in working for Tri-City and he advised me to fill out an application. I did and I was hired on as a helper in the fall of 1972.

I quickly learned the basics and moved up through the ranks. I became a journeyman electrician followed by superintendent. After eight years, they asked me to come into the office as a project manager, where I also learned to estimate. I tell people I'm an electrician by trade, because when I go on a job site I know what I'm looking at. Later, I became a department manager, then division manager, and later a division vice president. Finally, after the situation with Encompass fifteen years ago, a few of us bought the company back. That's how I became a partner in Tri-City.

Forty-six years is a long time. But it's been a good ride. There'll always be peaks and valleys in the construction business, so when we have slow times we get a chance to catch our breath. We need to be prepared for those times though, and if we're not, we're going to find ourselves wishing we had. Eventually things get better, and then we need to find the help to get the work done – to make hay while the sun shines, so to speak. That's why I like the word flexible: we need to adjust with the times. Times are good right now, but we've been through some pretty rough ones, too.

Keeping Good People

It's simple. If we treat employees, managers, associates, and clients as we would like to be treated, they'll stay with us for a long time. That is the Golden Rule, and that is Tri-City's golden rule as well. I believe that if we create a family atmosphere where people want to come to work and feel good

> about being here, we will be successful. After all,
> people want and need to belong to something. Our
> track record proves that approach works because
> we have so many employees who stayed with Tri-
> City for twenty-five years or more.
>
> **Buddy**

2

The Founder

When I first got to know Buddy, I could see right away he was well respected and fair with people. And he expected people, especially our clients, to be fair with him, too. To Buddy, it was a two-way street. He was one of those guys who led by example: first by coming to work on time every day (and he was here *early*). I still get here at 6:00 a.m. because Buddy would always be here early. He used to arrive in his site work clothes, even though he was head of the company. Later on, he switched to a coat and tie.

Buddy always burned the candle at both ends. He was very focused and he knew he wanted to build a business, which is the reason Tri-City is what it is today. He is also a very polished person, and a very analytical person. After he gets input from various areas, he will analyze, research, and go on to make a good decision. He's also been a good mentor to me and I've learned a lot from him through all these years.

One of Buddy's signature comments is, "Work smarter, not harder." Well, Buddy worked *really* hard, and that's how he made this organization what it is today. No one gets ahead by not being ahead of the game. If we get a jump on things in the early morning, which are the best hours in my opinion, we'll think clearer and get a lot more done.

Buddy wanted to grow the company and Paula wanted to help him. He wanted to build a business, not just be a subcontractor, so they pushed through to the top. Today, Tri-City is a force to be reckoned with. Today, we're the premier electrical contractor in Florida.

A Volatile Subject

I remember when John Bonner was outside filling his propane truck and somehow a spark set off the gas and blew him right out of the cab. When I got there, his skin was literally falling off his body. They helicoptered him to the hospital, and after that, Buddy said we were done with propane. We went to propane to economize, but obviously, it was way too dangerous.

Then there were those salvaged copper wire fishing trips. One time we were way out in the Gulf from Clearwater, and I was the designated money collector for the pot. The competition was whoever caught the largest edible fish by the end of the day would get the largest share of the prize. Well, half way through the day I leaned over the rail of the boat and saw my wallet that should have been in my pocket, floating past the boat. I hung way over the side and barely managed to fish it out of the sea. The guys said it was a good thing I got it, because if I hadn't, they would've thrown me overboard too.

David Beasley - Former Vice President, Tri City Electrical Contractors

3

Our Kind of Shop

Disney World was a huge project for Orlando at the time: far more than the city had ever seen. And through the years of its development, the unions had established a real stronghold as their primary source of construction. Seven years later however, when Disney was more or less complete, the unions needed something else to do. Having geared up all those years for Disney's big projects, they found themselves out of work and there were precious few big jobs to be had. Whatever large projects were out there, they wanted them. So, when Tri-City started to land larger commercial projects such as McNamara Pontiac, they took notice. They knew Tri-City was a force to be reckoned with.

In response, they made a run at us from time to time, and occasionally solicited our employees right in our front yard. In fact, on a couple of occasions they gathered at the end of Lorraine Drive, just down the road from our front door, handing out flyers to our employees hoping to organize them. But Tri-City has a better deal than the unions, which is why our employees stay right here. We're an open-shop contractor and we'll always be that way.

We have excellent benefits, a strong apprenticeship program, paid vacations, paid holidays, and company functions where we recognize our top performers. That's what keeps our company on top. The unions had their place years ago, but it's tough for them now. Fortunately, as Orlando grew, the pressure on the unions lessened.

***

Apprentices are critical to our prosperity as a company, and identifying potential journeymen starts with the new hires. Once they're on board, we look for what I call a "fire in the belly" attitude. When we see they have that, it's clear he or she wants to grow personally and grow with the company. They don't have to have a college degree. If they can read, write, do basic math, *and* have a fire in their belly, Tri-City will give them every opportunity. That's what happened with me because that's what Tri-City is all about: growth and a path to a good career. As the old Army slogan goes, "Be all you can be." That means if you work hard and show you want to succeed, you will succeed. Our company is laced with people who have been here thirty or thirty-five years because they've been given an opportunity to grow.

Fire in the belly is very important, but there is something else almost as important – people skills. You may be all you can be, but if you lack the ability to relate to people in a positive way, it will be hard to succeed. This company requires a lot of team effort to make things work.

People skills are not taught, they are learned. You have to learn to develop those skills as part of a company with diverse backgrounds and personalities. It doesn't matter if you're the best electrician in the world: if you don't have good interactive skills with others, or can't move forward with other people, you won't work out.

4

Family Culture

People like to work for a company that looks out for its employees. They enjoy being part of a successful company and want to contribute to that success. Tri-City recognizes the basic human need of being part of a group, and that seems to be rare in our industry. More often than not, companies operate with the mentality of providing as few benefits as possible, but just enough to keep the employee with them. We're the opposite. When someone hears about our company from one of our employees, and how good it is to work for Tri-City, it gives us real credibility. When a guy who just started working with us hears all those good reports, he thinks, "There must be something to this. I think I'll hang around to find out."

Papa Eidel was just like Buddy when it came to people skills. Papa was just as concerned about my family and me as he was about how

Papa's 80th Birthday

things went at work. I'd see him in the hall and after he said good morning he'd ask in his German accent, "How are you doing? And how is your Missus?" That is the Eidel culture, and it's been there from the very beginning.

Here's another way to put it: the U.S. Bureau of Labor Statistics shows the average turnover rate for the construction industry over a three-year period is 58 percent. By comparison, Tri-City's turnover rate for the same period averages 25 percent. That means our turnover rate is significantly lower than the national rate. There's a good reason for that.

Papa also helped our morale in other unique ways. In the early days of the business, we collected all the scrap copper we could from various jobs. Employees brought it back to the headquarters, where we had a special fireplace, a kiln of sorts, that Papa built. He was in charge of burning the insulation off the copper, and when it was done he sold it to a local scrap yard. Every year around September we took some of our employees on a fishing trip and paid for it with the "copper money fund." Everybody was motivated to collect all the copper they could to go on that fishing trip. And like any good incentive program, the more copper they gathered the better the trip!

A Loving Surrogate

When I was seven, my mom (who was single) moved us to Florida. She got a job at Tri-City and later met and married Buddy Eidel. I now refer to Buddy as dad, although I used to call him my stepfather. My biological father died many years ago, so Buddy became the most influential father figure for my sister, Stacia, and me.

I was eight when I first met Buddy and I thought he was a real nice guy. I liked him from the get-go and he treated my mom very well. Buddy had three daughters, so we were kind of like the Brady Bunch although they didn't' live with us.

When I talk with my friends, they tell me about all the bad things that happened to them growing up. But I didn't have any of that. Buddy and my mom provided a good, solid home for me. There was no doubt that they were there for us. Whenever anything was going on with sports and such, they were both there for me. And when I screwed up, Buddy wasn't happy about it. He'd discipline me for it, but he was still always there.

When I reached my twenties, Buddy told me about the electrical business. "The electrical contracting business," he said, "is like dancing with a gorilla." I asked him how. "As long as you keep dancing with the gorilla, everything is fine," he said. "But when you stop dancing, he'll tear you apart and eat you up." Of course, he was talking about clients, suppliers, employees, or the tax people. As long as you keep on top of things, the business will be fine. But if you let it go, it will all go downhill.

When I was eleven, I caught a hammerhead shark at Vero Beach and I wanted to get it stuffed by a taxidermist. I brought it home and stuck it in the outside freezer, but I know it drove him nuts because it was a nasty, smelly, fishy shark. Buddy tried to get a taxidermist, but at the time we were a middle-class family without the kind of money for that kind of service. He never found one, and that shark stayed in the freezer for over a year until I got rid of it. Then Buddy went out and bought me a shark's jaw to take its place.

When I was twelve, I remember him coming home one day and I was being a jerk. I was pouting like a typical pre-teen and it ticked him off. Finally, he said, "Listen Scott, I deal with assholes all day and I don't want to come home to one, too." When I reached my thirties, I looked back and had to laugh because he was right.

I worked for Buddy at the warehouse in my early twenties making fiberglass light encasements for attics. At the time, I really wanted a Mazda RX-7, but I had to drive a Camaro that was really a piece of junk. Well, Buddy had a vehicle repair shop at the company. So, one morning he took my Camaro in the shop while I was working and told me to pick it up in the afternoon. At the end of the day, he poked his head in my area and said, "hey, your car is done." We walked outside and he said, "here it is." But I didn't see my car. "Where is it?" I asked. "Right there in front of you," he replied, pointing to a brand new Mazda RX-7 parked in front of us. Then he handed me the keys.

I was ecstatic, and I drove that car for twelve years. That was a tremendous thing, but he did things like that for all the kids.

Despite their wealth, both of my parents are very humble, down-to-earth people. They also have a certain class about them and never talk down to anyone. I've tried to emulate that in my life. Now that I'm older, at the ripe age of fifty-four, they've become two of my best friends. I talk to them about many things, and I consider them two of the smartest people I know.

Scott Haffner – Our Son

Scott

My stepson, Scott, was quite a mischievous and athletic boy. When he was in junior high, I built a skateboard ramp and all the kids in the neighborhood used it. When one of his buddies let fly with colorful language, he told them to knock it off because his mom was inside, and she did not like "locker room talk."

Paula used to take Scott and his friends to football practice and pick them up afterward. One particularly hot summer day on the way home in the car, she asked the kids what in the world the awful smell was. They all hollered that it was Joey's feet. It was so bad they had to roll down the windows.

One night when Scott's grandparents babysat him, he decided to sneak out of the house. But Grandpa understood what was going on, so he locked him out of the house. Scott wound up sleeping in the car inside the garage.

Scott has always been sensitive and very attentive to his parents. To illustrate, here's a verbatim copy of the toast he gave in my honor in 2018:

"Buddy, I wish you a wonderful Father's Day! But more than that, I want you to know how much you are appreciated by your children because you are the "glue" that holds our family together. In Webster's Dictionary, next to the definition of "father," there should be a picture of you because you epitomize what a father should be. I want you to know that all the things you've done for us kids has not gone unnoticed. We all are very grateful and love you very much! So, on this day, I raise my glass and toast Helmuth Leo Eidel, the best father ever!"

Buddy

5

Best Practices

What helps transform a small company into a large business? Structure. Which means careful, thought-out policies and procedures must be in place to allow for growth. That's an area where Paula and Buddy worked hard and worked together. Over time, they adopted logical policies and procedures that everyone knew about and agreed to. When everyone was on board, those policies became part of the company culture. When that was done, we started pushing to the next level: growing from a small subcontractor to a full-blown business. To accomplish that, and help me become a better people person, Buddy sent me to numerous training courses. I have a business management degree from Rollins College, and several certificates from Dale Carnegie training courses, which Buddy and Paula attended with me.

Of course, we've had challenges along the way. I've noticed that every time we jump the track, such as taking on a project that turns bad for one reason or another, we can trace the problem back to a policy or procedure that was not followed. For example, in any construction company a job cost program is one of its most important tools. If a program can break down the project into small pieces, so we can keep our eyes on each piece, the project will come together nicely. If not, it can be disastrous, which is what happened to us a couple of times in the early years. Today, we have an *excellent* job cost program, and I credit Buddy for developing that. If we follow all the steps of our program or policy, we're almost certain to be successful. It's a simple formula, but the hard part is crafting a good model and sticking close to the guidelines.

We have an early indicator, or warning program. There's no name for it, but it's an integral part of our job costing system. If a problem is detected early, the solution will be a whole lot easier to implement. Maybe we can't fix 100 percent of it, but we can reduce the negative impact quite a bit. But if we find the mistake when the job is almost done, it's probably too late to do anything about it. There is no autopilot in our business, and we all need to pay close attention. I'm a stickler on that, because when we pay close attention we can see all the little bumps and bruises before they become big ones.

At Tri-City, we apply the adage, "What gets measured, gets done." When we inform our employees what our expectations are, we can measure their progress. I'm happy to say we have an excellent track record on that one. For example, we know how long it takes to run 100 feet of conduit, and we also know it takes longer to run 100 feet of conduit in a 50-foot high ceiling than it does here on the ground. There are always lots of variables, but we make it our business to know what they are. Knowing every detail is part of what drives down job costs, which helps the manager know how the job is progressing. We measure, get the criterion, then explain, and measure the results. That's what it's all about at the end of every month, and that's what makes the difference in our bottom line.

6

Divide and Multiply

Early on, Buddy realized that diversification would lead to success. When I say diversify, I mean having multiple divisions, or profit centers. Today, we have numerous centers: residential, service, multi-family, and commercial to name a few. Many companies don't create divisions with clean lines of responsibility, but instead specialize only in one area, or place all their products or services in one pool.

Our divisions took shape over time, and as a result it really allowed us to grow. In our industry, not all market segments expand at the same time. For example, the commercial market may be strong, perhaps through government spending, while another segment like individual homes may be slow. Offering many areas of expertise can balance the ebb and flow of market trends and smooth out the production curve. Otherwise, if a company focuses on one segment of the market and that segment doesn't do well, guess what? You're not doing well at all.

The decision to diversify and specialize was not a cognitive decision: it evolved. If the demand was there, we could choose to push into that market. Of course, each of those markets has special needs, so that's the reason Buddy calls them profit centers. Each one has to make it or break it without depending on the rest of the company.

7

A Ready Aftermarket

Often, when we complete a project, we get called back later for repairs or warranty. Then, after the warranty runs out or time passes, the same company might call us back to do more repair work. That's because we know the building and the systems, which was a main driver in developing our service department. That profit center was a byproduct of the years we were owned by Encompass, when it pushed all its companies to provide after-sales service. What developed from that income stream was another profit center called special projects. Those are nice, fast-paced jobs that can be anywhere. So, we had to be equipped and staffed to move fast, kind of like a rapid deployment force for the electrical contracting industry. If we aren't ready, we can't do those jobs well, or maybe not at all. Again, our diverse approach provided the systems, the strategy, and the means for further success.

Speaking of diversifying, that's how I wound up doing residential and multi-family homes. That profit center has grown into a fairly large segment for us. I travel all over Florida and the Southeastern U.S. to manage large multi-family projects. It's interesting that I can count on both hands the number of clients, or contracting companies, in my sphere of influence. I have a lot of repeat business and I take care of those customers first.

Sometimes it costs a lot of money to take care of a client, and when it does, most of the time it's not our fault. Nevertheless, I want their contract the next time, and the next. If I don't make them happy on *this* job, it won't matter how cheap my price is on the next bid because I won't get their business. They'll take my low bid and run it by my competitor. You've got to do what it takes on the current project, and that will get you invited to the next party. Of course, I'm talking about general contractors here.

Sometimes our industry can be very combative. My approach is, if we do what we're supposed to do, we can stay out of head-to-head competition. I'll continue to do everything I can to make the general contractor's job as smooth as possible. Having said that, nothing in this business is easy. I remember a time when we all sat round the conference table discussing current events. The conversation got a bit heated, and at one point Buddy sat up and said, "Listen guys, if it was easy, everybody would be doing it."

He was right. The electrical contracting business is tough. Competition is tough. Markets can be brutal. Clients can be difficult. After you estimate your work, and the ink on the contract is dry, it's still just an educated guess. We have a great philosophy for our business, and great systems to take much of the guesswork out of the process. We give our managers the tools they need to manage their jobs. We've done the best we can and that's why we're successful.

Treat Your Job Like You Own It

Paula was my stepmom, so my sisters and I mostly spent time with her and dad on weekends. She did everything she could to make us feel at home and kept up with family traditions like Christmas cookies and all our birthdays. She really made us feel comfortable, like true members of a large family. My dad worked a lot of course, because his business was very important to him. He went to all our functions, but the main thing was his company.

When each of us turned forty, we all took a family vacation somewhere. It took a lot of planning on Paula's part, but she managed to arrange activities for everyone. We went to places like Hawaii, Mexico, or Colorado, and she did a real bang-up job of planning those events. The best vacation was the first one, when we went to Hawaii for the 2000 New Year. It was special because I'd never been to Hawaii and everyone thought the world would end at midnight because of Y2K. But, of course, nothing happened at midnight. We didn't have to use the candles or flashlights the hotel provided, and we didn't have to avoid the elevator and walk downstairs to be safe. The trip was just a lot of good memories.

I got along pretty well with all my siblings. Stacia and Scott were not around as much: Stacia was older and in high school doing her thing, and Scott played football. But my blood siblings, Tammy and Bethany, mostly got along with each other.

I laugh at the memory of dad when he was in his element. During Christmastime, we usually went to a German restaurant in Lake Mary called Hollerbach's Willow Tree Café. They had live music and dad would be feeling really good, so he'd sing along with the band: "*Eins, Zwo, Drei!*" It reminded him of growing up in his German family.

My dad was a very hard-working man who taught me what a good day's work meant and how to go above and beyond. He was a very honest man. Even if his name was dragged through the dirt (even if it wasn't true), he still picked the high road.

To this day, family is one of the most important things to him. He sometimes got upset when my sister and I didn't behave because family was so important to him. Paula made sure the family had things to do and that the family stayed together. She is a social butterfly and she's the glue that kept us together. She was also a great support for my dad because he was a worker bee, while she was the one who reached out to people. In that way she was also responsible for his success, because she brought people in and held social functions and such.

Because of my upbringing, I always gave 100 percent to my job as well as to my husband. I'm very much like my dad because sometimes my work has become all consuming, and at times it has affected my family life. I always wanted to leave work at the end of the day with my head held high, knowing I did the very best I could. Although I never owned a business, I treated each job as if it was my own.

Joyce Rose - Our Daughter

JOYCE

Our daughter Joyce was an adventurer and traveler who always welcomed new experiences. In junior high, she and Tammy experimented with modeling and beauty pageants. It was a great experience because it taught them poise, good grooming, and how to present oneself. Joyce was also a cheerleader in school, but her childhood dream was to attend Oral Roberts University. While we could hardly afford it, we made sure that's where she went to school.

When we had four children in college at the same time, we joked every time the phone rang: we were afraid one of them would ask for more money. We always thought we would be rich once they graduated.

After graduating from Oral Roberts, Joyce went directly from Oklahoma to Chicago. That's where she is today, and she loves it. Even though she's far away from Florida, it has been fun for us to go back and forth to Chicago, a place we call "Toddlin' Town." Nearing retirement now, Joyce and her husband bought a condo in Sunny Isles, Florida where they

> go for the winter months. Happily, we see all our children often.
>
> **Buddy**

Jack Olmstead

1

Getting to Know the Boss

I grew up in Indianapolis, where my father-in-law was president of Watson-Flagg Electric Co., which is part of Fischbach & Moore, a heavy construction commercial and electrical company. He encouraged me to enter an electrical apprenticeship program, but at the time it was highly competitive and hard to get into. I didn't make the first round but got in after the second attempt. I went on to become a journeyman, a superintendent, and a project manager for Robbins Electric in Indianapolis. I went on to work for WESCO supply for a couple of years until I received an offer to join Long Electric as its field operations manager. I stayed with them from 1980 through 1995, working my way to vice president and Indianapolis division manager.

In 1994, I used a headhunter, Dolly Lee from Atlanta, to hire a project manager for our Indianapolis office. As we discussed our needs, I happened to ask her what was going on around Atlanta and other areas. She told me a gentleman with Tri-City Electrical Contractors was looking for a division manager for his Tampa office. It was cold in Indiana and I always wanted to live in Florida. What pushed me more was the recruiter kept encouraging me to send in my resume. At first, I was reluctant and didn't have much interest. But after five or more conversations, I stopped by Kinkos and faxed her my resume.

I flew to Florida in February of 1995, arriving on a Daytona 500 race day weekend. That meant I couldn't find a room anywhere. I finally landed one at midnight, and worried that I would miss my interview with Buddy the next morning. But I made it right on time, at 8:00 a.m. Sunday at a Perkins Restaurant near Tri-City headquarters.

We hit it off immediately. I mean, the guy was amazing. I just really liked him. He brought me back to the office to meet then-vice president David Beasley, and their CFO. Then we talked about the position in their Tampa office.

Talking with Buddy was almost unreal because he was too good, too sincere: I have to admit I was a little skeptical. I was also concerned about Florida contractors. I'd heard a lot about people going to Florida to find businesses weren't really on the up-and-up. There was no internet at the time, so I couldn't pull up any data about Buddy Eidel and Tri-City, but I had a good CPA friend who called around Florida for me. He checked clients, former clients, and other relations he knew there. He couldn't find anything at all that was negative about Buddy Eidel. It was all positive. He said that guy was a real jewel; an honest, hard-working businessman who started his company from nothing and made it into a successful enterprise.

Nevertheless, when I talked with Buddy later on, I said I wasn't sure I was ready to accept the position. I had recently divorced and would be leaving my teenage son and daughter behind with their mother. Buddy wanted to make me an offer that day, saying he had to replace the Tampa manager who was having issues. He wanted fresh blood from the outside because he didn't have anyone inside the company to put in that position.

2

Taking the Leap

We continued to talk over the next few months and I even flew down a couple more times. We went to the Tampa office where Buddy introduced me as a prospect for the division manager. I kept liking that guy more and more. I also found out Paula was from Indianapolis, so when we went to dinner we talked about her old Indianapolis high school and Butler University, which was one of the Indiana basketball powerhouses. We finally decided I would come on board.

I gave my thirty day notice to Long Electric, Inc., and on Monday April 3, 1995 I started work at Tri-City. I didn't take a single day off between jobs because I couldn't wait to get started. Long Electric didn't want me to leave, but I said, "Listen, I want to wake up every day in Florida, and I want to work for Buddy Eidel."

He picked me up at the Orlando International Airport that morning. It was funny because when I came out of the jet way, Buddy told me my clothes had already arrived at the office via UPS. I could tell he was very happy to see me.

I also wanted to work for Buddy because he had high morals and standards and he was very polite. There wasn't any cockiness or arrogance about him at all, and I was completely comfortable with him. Buddy is the kind of boss who will let you do your job. That was my first impression of him, and I really saw myself helping him do whatever had to be done.

There were around ninety-five people in the Tampa office and over four hundred fifty in Altamonte Springs. Originally, I was supposed to be trained at the main office. But soon after I arrived, Buddy said: "Listen, we need to go to Tampa now. There's some trouble over there and we have to solve some problems." He was managing Tampa in addition to the main company, so he needed to get me going as fast as possible. In the early days, he spent a lot of time there and Paula sometimes came and stayed with him. She was also anxious to get something buttoned-up and get Buddy back to the main office and home every night.

He walked me through various jobs, went over the financial systems, and everything else I needed to know. It was hands-on right there and he was with me all the time so I could do things correctly right out of the starting block.

***

Buddy and Paula are an amazing couple: It was almost as if I was friends with the Winter Park mayor and his wife. They have a lot of friends, are very influential, and grew a massive and highly successful business. When you saw them together, they were just a powerhouse. But they were also very kind, without that rich person arrogance, or "I'm better than anybody else" attitude. Buddy was out there on the job with you whether you were shoveling or doing anything else, and you knew it. Buddy liked to use the term, "Let's go stomp around on some jobs to see what's going on."

On Positive Attitudes

I always thought I could do whatever I dreamed. If I felt like I could do something, I usually wound up doing it. The key was not allowing any negatives to creep in to my thinking to disrupt my problem-solving process. No matter what the problem, I looked for a solution instead.

Buddy

3

The Apprentices

Tri-City has what may be considered the best apprenticeship package among all the state-approved programs. But it didn't arrive at that point without a lot of work. Here's the story.

NECA is a strong organization of union members that has always excelled with its training programs. Having gone through a union apprenticeship program myself, I still found it superior in many ways. The trainers don't put up with apprentices taking a cavalier approach. Apprentices had few rights. They couldn't quit a contractor, and if they did they were out of the program. They had to do what they were told for four long years. In reality, the apprenticeship program was a highly disciplined organization with very little tolerance for tardiness or absenteeism. But once they graduated, they were a journeyman — one of the rank and file.

The Florida ABC also has apprenticeship programs, and Tri-City was involved in the Tampa Bay area training. Buddy was also involved in the FEAT training program, which was sponsored by the Florida Association of Electrical Contractors. Buddy and his dad were big supporters and advocates of the apprenticeship programs ever since Tri-City went to the Joint Apprenticeship Training Committee (JATC), a union sponsored program. All that involvement meant Buddy knew apprentices were the future of the industry, so Tri-City supported the program and offered it to all qualified new hires.

However, like NECA's programs, there was a cost to send apprentices to the school and not all contractors wanted to spend the money. Nevertheless, for several years, Tri-City sent apprentices to the JATC and Buddy even served on the JATC board for a while. Not only was it expensive, it proved to be somewhat complicated because once apprentices became journeymen, union shops zeroed in to recruit them to their own companies. That meant Buddy spent all that time, effort, and money training his employees only to have them absorbed by union shops.

The story continues.

After a few years, ABC received approval from the U.S. Department of Labor to start its own "indentured apprenticeship program." Later, FAEC started a separate electrical apprenticeship program of its own and named it FEAT. (Florida Electrical Apprenticeship and Training). David Beasley became very active with FEAT and served on its board to promote the program. The FEAT program was every bit as rigorous as NECA's training. Rumor has it that a FEAT board member made a point of telling new apprentices they had to work in the daytime and attend classes at night, and the only excuse for absence was a death in the family — their own.

Rumors aside, the numbers showed how effective the program was. By the summer of 1994, Tri-City had registered thirty-four new apprentices for the FEAT summer term and eighty-four new apprentices for the fall term. That brought the combined total for residential and commercial apprentices to one hundred ninety-eight, making Tri-City the number one sponsor for apprentices in the program.

Tri-City was, and continues to be, a big contributor to FEAT. The organization provides good, qualified training while meeting the national criterion sanctioned by the government. That makes FEAT a bona fide program that helps Tri-City train and retain quality electricians.

It is interesting to note that back in Indianapolis, I had to fight my way into the union training program: about four hundred of us competed for forty positions! But, down here we actually have trouble getting people interested, or committed, to attend school two nights a week. We almost have to shove them in the door. Now, we don't pay them to attend classes, but we pay for everything else, including books. We figure their time is on them because classes take place after work hours. Once they graduate from those programs, they've got something no one else has. If they have fire in their belly, they'll attend those classes.

Today, we develop our own programs and work with Rollins College or similar institutions that offer the programs as part of their curriculum. Rollins professor Dr. Rick Bommelje conducts supervisory training at our Charles J. Eidel Training Building. We've also done training in Tampa, along with other programs like Dale Carnegie courses to keep employees up to speed with their people skills.

Buddy was very big into the Fails Management Institute, which helped set up and monitor the earlier training at Tri-City (the organization now calls itself FMI since the word "Fails" doesn't send a very positive message). Buddy wanted everybody trained, qualified, and signed off to meet all the requirements and have every opportunity to grow in their job.

They Called Him "Buddy"

I first met Buddy when I was a federal prosecutor from Washington D.C. I was twenty-six-years-old and we were at a party where an acquaintance, who later became my law partner, introduced us. That was 1973, and our economy was in a bad economic slump. I immediately liked him. As a prosecutor who faced the citrus barons of Florida, I'd heard about Tri-City and was very impressed

I also heard Buddy got up at 2:30 a.m. to check the Dodge Report for pending work through contractors, so he could get a leg up on the prospects. At the time, his company was touch and go as to whether it would make it. Regardless, his hard work pulled him out of it and Tri-City went on to become one of the top twenty-five electrical contractors in the country.

My wife, Jane, and Paula, play bridge together as well as golf at the Interlachen Country Club. We have been a foursome of friends for over forty years.

Something few people know about Buddy is that the Harvard program he attended inspired him to commission someone to develop code for a project bidding program. The program assured that Tri-City had dotted the i's and crossed the t's before submitting a bid. Buddy was going after some very big jobs at the time, such as jails and large convention centers with 25,000 seats, so it had to be right the first time.

Buddy had around twelve or fourteen projects going at once, which is what he tried to maintain. So when the bid was made, the program prevented mistakes like under bidding or over bidding, which either way could cost them millions.

The day they sold their business to the roll-up corporation, my wife and I joined Buddy and Paula at a nice Italian restaurant. I knew the owner, and in fact I had represented him in a legal matter, but he wasn't there that night. His maître d' was there, and he kept making a big deal over the people at the next table. I guess they were some kind of celebrities, but the problem was he just kept ignoring us. Well, I almost told him that the guy next to me, Buddy, just sold his company for eight figures or so, and why the hell are you treating us like bums off the street? But he kept ignoring us. Anyway, Buddy didn't seem to mind much, and I managed to keep my mouth shut.

Later, when Buddy and the others at Tri-City tried to get the business back from bankruptcy court, Lance Walker, the owner of Walker Construction Company, heard about it. Lance offered to send a $1 million check to Buddy to help out. It was like, "Hey Buddy, here's a million dollars ... there's no interest, no paperwork, no nothing." Buddy didn't need it at the time, but I believe that grand gesture will remain in our memories for good.

We always enjoy going out with Buddy and Paula, and we always like being together because we laugh a lot. Buddy is also very attuned to what's going on

Paula – President of ICC Ladies Golf Association – 1990

in the world politically, economically, and so forth. He's also vigilant when it comes to the stock market.

He and Paula are moving to a new condo soon, and I went there when they were building it. I came across several workmen in the garage bringing stuff up to their apartment and they all called him "Buddy," not "Mr. Eidel" or anything so formal. I thought it was great.

If it weren't for Buddy, there wouldn't be 1,200 Tri-City employees, there wouldn't be 1,200 home mortgages being paid, or at least that many kids going to college. What began in a garage in 1959 has developed into what it is today. It's a textbook story. It's the American Dream.

Harrison T. "Butch" Slaughter Jr. - Florida Bar Certified Criminal Trial Attorney

4

Boosting the Industry

Today, Tri-City belongs to a six-company organization called the PAG (Peer Advisory Group) with some of the original Electrical Quality Circle members. We share information with each other and similar companies throughout the U.S. Early on, Buddy took David Beasley, me, and a few others to visit different companies where we learned their best practices and unique ways of building pre-fabricated electrical components, and the special tools utilized in the process. We didn't compete with those companies because we were all separated geographically or strategically, so we could share financial information and most everything else. If one of the members had a customer in another member's area, they would help take care of the customer's needs. The best part was mingling with people from another company in the same industry without the usual barriers.

We continue to be one of ABC's primary supporters, and they support us as well. In addition to ABC's programs, we provide our own awards ceremonies to recognize many of our employees for their accomplishments. For their part, ABC forms a committee consisting of architects, engineers and others to provide unbiased judgment of the various projects to determine which company receives high marks for the year. The results are a big deal in our industry, and we celebrate that every year. Additionally, almost every month ABC will have a social where all members get together.

There is always some kind of training going on at Tri-City, such as a ten-week supervisory training program. We also send our project managers to a class to hear from one of our senior project managers. Often students come from all over our industry as well. We like to be the one in charge to steer the process, even if we're training some of our competitor's employees. In the big picture, it's good for our industry because when everyone is better at what they do, everyone makes more money.

***

In 1998, while I was still division manager in Tampa, Buddy called the management team to the conference room in Altamonte Springs and announced he had sold the company. When I heard that, you could've knocked me over with a feather. There were about nine of us in that room, and from the looks on the other faces they all felt the same. David Beasley was there, so Buddy had probably told him before we arrived, since David already had a shocked look on his face. I had zero idea that announcement was coming.

The first thing that went through my mind was, "man, I came to Tri-City to work for Buddy. I gave up a good job in a good position. And now he'll be gone next week?"

But then he told us he's not really leaving for a while. I think the term he used was, "Nothing's going to change. Everything is going to keep going like it is."

He said a group owned by a guy named Jonathan Ledecky put a deal together to buy electrical contractor companies, and all seven of the Quality Circle members were being purchased.

We found out that for several months our CFO, Chuck McFarland, had been working in confidence with Buddy and Paula to sell the company and make sure Buddy was being treated fairly by Ledecky. They developed financials and faxed reams of documents in the middle of the night. Things like that. Obviously, Chuck couldn't say anything.

I was happy for Buddy, but I was very concerned about what would happen to all of us. And what's really going to happen to Tri-City? I'd never been involved in something like that before.

On Social Responsibility

In the spirit of giving back to the community, Tri-City has increasingly contributed as much as possible to numerous charities during the good times and lean ones. Substantial donations were made, or continue to be made, to organizations like the University of Central Florida Library Enrichment Fund, Junior Achievement, Special Olympics, Shriner's Hospital, Boy Scouts of Central Florida, Heart of United Way, American Red Cross, Orlando Museum of Art, the Florida Symphony, and Boys Town, among others.

More recently, the company made significant donations to the Central Florida Chapter of the Children's Home Society of Florida, Life Path Hospice of Tampa, Give Kids the World organization, Metropolitan Ministries of Tampa, Habitat for

Humanity, the Florida Children's Hospital Foundation, and Inspire of Central Florida.

More sizable donations have been made to the National Center for Construction Education and Research. Tri-City also donated time and material to build part of Seminole State College of Florida to house the apprenticeship program. Of course, Tri-City also helps its own family. In 2005, the Tri-City Scholarship Fund (renamed the Tri-City Chuck McFarland Scholarship after his untimely death in 2014) was established. Scholarships are awarded every year to qualified high school seniors who are children or grandchildren of Tri-City employees. Each student can receive up to $2,500 per year for up to four years of undergraduate study, for a maximum of $10,000. To date, the scholarship has disbursed more than $340,000 to nearly forty students.

Much more goes on behind the scenes, such as employees in difficult circumstances. It started with Buddy and has continued through the years. For example, the wife of one of our electricians was critically ill and needed her husband at home. When his co-workers heard of the situation and realized the loss of wages would be an added burden for his family, they passed the hat. Several of them donated one day of their own vacation time so he could spend three weeks with his wife and not lose his income. That is a touching example of the culture of Tri-City.

Jane Hodges

5

Consolidation

Many years ago, I was involved with a Midwestern company that
went bankrupt largely due to the officers being involved in a bid rigging
scheme. Could my great life with a great job and a great group of people
come to an end as quickly? As Buddy continued discussing the sale of
the company, questions kept coming up in my mind: "What about my
future? What about our employees' futures?" Buddy said he would grant
stock to some of the management group as part of the purchase deal, and
we would have an option to buy more in the future. It was very generous
of Buddy to grant a portion of his stock to us. That all sounded good,
but I still wondered.

After the debris settled somewhat, Buddy asked me to fly to Phoenix
with him to attend a meeting with a few other CEOs in the new group.
There was Charlie Walker of Walker Engineering, Rollie Stevenson from
Town & Country, Steve Gubin from Wilson Electric (members of the
original Quality Circle) and the main person, Jonathan Ledecky, the one
who started the whole thing. He turned out to be a dynamic Harvard
graduate with a very interesting background in the financial industry.

***

After Ledecky's organization purchased Tri-City in the roll-up
acquisition, we became part of Consolidated Capital Corporation. Not
long after, to better identify the kind of business it was, it was renamed
as Building One Services. Regardless of the name, those of us involved
in the conglomerate kept right on working as if nothing had changed, as
Ledecky had promised.

In due time, because the shareholders (our real owners) weren't
satisfied with Building One's profitability, Jonathan was compelled to
acquire more companies to expand the business model. That was the
trend in the late nineties, and roll-up investors thought the best way to

greater profitability was to spend more money. That's what Jonathan did, and in short order the group was renamed Encompass. By then, Jonathan had sold his interest and moved on to other things. Smart guy.

A couple of years later, we had grown to about three hundred companies across the country, contributing $3.7 billion in total revenues. We'd also merged with Group MAC, another roll-up consisting of HVAC contractors. Those were the days when M&A was the big thing and everybody rocked and rolled by acquiring more and more. Collectively, we spent a fortune on rebranding initiatives from all the acquisitions and corporate name changes. What they did was buy well-known and popular names, then merged them all into a national brand. The successful roll-ups did not do that: they maintained the original names. A better idea would have been to keep it "Tri-City Electrical Contractors, Inc., a Division of Encompass Services."

Corporate leaders were in the habit of flying us out to meet new principals, hear some new announcement, or undergo special training, usually at the last minute. They also created a university in Houston, where we were expected to send different levels of management for week-long corporate training programs. Some of the things they taught in Houston were nothing more than role-playing games or "high-level" instruction by various corporate trainers they had hired for certain initiatives. We had to sit and listen to what we, as electrical and mechanical contractors, did not think were good ideas at the time.

Key people from companies, like Polaroid or Shell Oil - executives with different visions, ran several of those meetings. They all worked from an ivory tower in Houston in five leased floors. We'd look around and shake our heads, amazed at how the money just flew out the windows for complete nonsense. I had trouble convincing some of our guys like David Beasley or Steve Pomeroy to participate in training for a week in Houston when they knew they could be at home doing their job and making money. They were right.

Several companies that weren't setting the world on fire when Encompass bought them suddenly found themselves with a higher bonding capacity. That meant these companies could bond all the work they wanted because they had the backing of the big corporation. Now that they had the biggest bankroll they'd ever seen, they went for bigger and bigger jobs, regardless of whether they had the expertise. For example, a couple of those companies landed a contract with an oil refinery. Though none of them were qualified, they (and Encompass) bled money trying to complete the projects. The same thing happened with a major entertainment company in California: Contractors without that kind of project experience presented credentials from Encompass and bagged the job. The result was a predictable failure.

I remember one meeting that took place two days after flights had resumed following the September 11 tragedy. We headed to Denver for another major, mandatory meeting with a group of presidents and other executives. The meeting turned out to be yet another idea that really made no sense. You could have heard a pin drop when they explained how we should get the general contractors and owners to forego the usual 10 percent retention, which would greatly increase cash flow. Then in a related topic someone said, "Well, if you don't make enough money on service, you just raise your price." Okay, I thought, if you can't get the work at $65 an hour, how are you going to collect $75 an hour? Things like that just didn't compute.

Encompass had become a mega organization that had outgrown its purpose. It also spent way too much money trying to find solutions for a shrinking cash flow. One time we were in Lakeland, Florida, looking at another potential acquisition. When we were ready to pull the trigger and start the due diligence, the top leaders sent an urgent message. "Reduce acquisitions! Reduce mergers!"

The organization was in a panic mode.

I remember what one of the Encompass board members told me when he came to town: "You know, there was a time when we were scared to death the former owners were going to leave. Then we got to the point where we were afraid they'd never go away. So, we started getting rid of some them."

6

Escape Plan

The whole roll-up model started to unravel. Money kept hemorrhaging but deals were still being cut. Since the bonding company tightened the flow of future bonds, we all had to compete for bonding and present a profit and cash flow sheet of expected returns. That meant sometimes we couldn't obtain a bond for a customer, and we lost the contract. A few contractors looked at us with a tear in their eye and said they couldn't give us the job because it would be too much of a risk. Like wartime, with all the changes going on in the industry, bonds were actually rationed, and we had to compete with other Encompass companies to get bonded for our local projects. Although we devised accurate bonding petitions and produced financials and calculations to prove we could do the job, it often was not good enough. We lost a couple of great projects in Tampa and a few more in Orlando. In our client's mind, if we (Encompass) went into Chapter 11, a form of bankruptcy that focuses on reorganization, we might not be around to finish the job. Nevertheless, we stayed in touch with customers, kept them informed of our progress, and somehow the contracts continued to trickle in.

Meanwhile, in other parts of the country, the corporation continued to fund the cost overruns. Decision-making went unchecked. Even Tri-City's revenue dropped quite a bit, to the point we had to lay off some of our employees. In our estimation, reduced capacity meant we could meet our actual business flow. While that was strategically correct, it was extremely painful for us, even if Encompass did come up with a few packages to help out. Worse yet, we had to lay off some of the good quality people we'd recently hired. Ultimately, Encompass became so unwieldy that (not surprisingly) it prepared to file for bankruptcy.

When it was obvious the ship was going down, Chuck McFarland, as chief master planner, Rance Borderick, and I, started to piece together a plan to take the company back. We absolutely did not want to watch Tri-

City go down with the rest. I met with Joe Ivey, then CEO of Encompass, and said we were interested in buying the company back. His response was buying it back was not possible because Tri-City had been a good company that performed well and made good money. He said there had been a few problems here and there, but we were earmarked to be part of the new, smaller (leaner and meaner?) Encompass once it shed the non-performing companies. But we could see down the road to what was going to happen. That wasn't where we wanted to go, so we decided to move ahead anyway.

We formed a separate, "New Tri-City Electrical Contracting Inc." on the side, with just enough differentiation in the name to be legal, but to let clients know we were essentially the same organization. We were free to do that because we had never signed a non-compete agreement before we were purchased. So we had that going for us. It gave us enough of an opening to create a legal entity that could feed work to the larger Encompass group.

After we formed the new company, we began to subcontract new business to the original Tri-City. Now there were two separate Tri-Citys, but we did it without violating any part of the original agreement. To be sure, we consulted with our attorneys to ensure it was legal before we made the move. There was no hidden agenda and we didn't try to keep it a secret. We just had to be careful how we contracted; that we didn't steal business from the former Tri-City and pass it on to the new Tri-City. It had to be new business only.

All the while, we maintained our good relationships with customers. David Beasley had already left the company by then, as well as a few others. They felt like we were on a downward trend and wanted to find another home before the market was flooded with talent. I didn't have a problem with that because I understood. We were building another company while trying to make the original one work, and that was pretty scary. It was also understandable because our revenue had dipped to about 40 percent of its normal volume.

In the meantime, FMI (Fails Management Inc.) was hired by Encompass to sell off some of the lesser-performing companies to create a leaner, meaner organization. Now the clarion call was shrink instead of acquire. Some of colleagues in the roll-up merger managed to buy back their companies. Continental Electric of Chicago, Town & Country, and Pomeroy Electric put deals together so they could continue to operate.

Although we were told we could not buy back our company, Tri-City was still being marketed to people who wanted in. An executive from FMI brought in different investors and we all sat around a conference table while they performed due diligence. They checked our profit and loss statements, project track record, bond history, and so forth. They went through our whole program of how we became who we were. On one occasion, after all the questions were answered, the prospective buyer said: "Hey, this is great. We'd love to own this company. You guys would be a great part of our portfolio."

That's when I piped up.

"Listen, there's something you need to know. We, our management group, want to buy the company back."

When they heard that, the curt reply was:

"Oh, well, if I had known that I probably wouldn't have come."

Then I continued:

"In fact, we want to buy the company so bad that we formed a new company to do the work, and if somebody else buys this company, we're going to pack up and take all the business with us, including the employees because we'll need them."

"Oh," he said. "We didn't know that."

One of the prospects was a big Wall Street executive who tried hard to muscle in on the deal. He and an electrical contractor friend in New York had formed an agreement to buy us. The investor was quite wealthy and he said we could come along for the ride and cooperate whether we wanted to or not. But we kept pushing him and others back until Encompass's time ran out.

7

Getting Buddy Back

We knew if bankruptcy actually happened we would have a good chance to put our plan into action. We had a friendly banker who could help us out, but he wasn't in a position to loan us what we needed without some strong collateral. So, we contacted Buddy. We asked him if we could borrow a little bit of capital to make a bid on the company. We also invited him back in, but not as an owner, if he'd be willing to help us. Of course, we said we'd pay him back. Buddy was still passionate about the company and he said he would help us figure something out.

Paula wanted to help us financially, but she didn't want Buddy immersed in the management of the company again. So, they came up with a good plan.

They pledged the buildings in Altamonte Springs and Tampa as collateral for our loan. It was a very good move on their part, and we couldn't have financed the deal without them. Later, Buddy told me a story about a rumor that had been going around at the time. He was at a restaurant in Winter Park and one of the guys he'd known for years walked up and said, "Hey, Buddy, I understand you're trying to put the band back together."

Well, yes and no.

Fortunately, we had a great bonding agent in Jacksonville, Tom Lobrano III, who also helped. He was good friends with Chuck McFarland, and they'd known each other for many years. When we were putting the deal together, the agent wrote a personal check for $250,000 and mailed it to Chuck. A note inside the envelope read, "This might help you a little bit." I couldn't believe that guy would just write a personal check to help us to get back on our feet and provide our bonding. But he did.

***

Armed with help from Buddy, the bonding agent, and our bank, we appeared at the bankruptcy court in Houston to bid for the company. Unless someone popped up with a better offer, our prospects looked good. Well, it nearly didn't work out.

A businessman from Lakeland, Florida, tried to elbow in at the last minute. He had formed a small organization that had managed to corral enough investors to make an offer. Now it came down to who made the strongest bid for the company. But before that guy could put in his bid, Buddy took him out into the hallway to have a serious conversation. He didn't threaten to break his knees or anything, but I heard later that Buddy told him point-blank if he bought the company out from under his people, he would make sure his Tri-City deal would not work out for him and that the New Tri-City would bring all the employees over as well as all the customers. In other words, the man would buy a company without key players, staff, and a client base. The man knew and respected Buddy, so he agreed to back out. Without a larger bid, the judge signed off on our purchase of the company.

When the gavel banged, the company was ours. Chuck and I caught the elevator, and we did belly bumps all the way to the ground floor.

When we got back to our headquarters in Altamonte Springs, several employees who heard the news had torn down the Encompass sign and tossed it in the trash. It was a glorious day.

We held a big meeting the next day and most of it was cheering and celebration. Now we were back on our own, and Buddy Eidel's legacy would continue.

I signed reams of documents on Feb. 27, 2003, and we officially took Tri-City back to a private company again. It was amazing how it all came together. The great thing was, we bought the company at a time when the market started to go back up. Later in 2003, it climbed like crazy. Here are excerpts from an article written later that year. It sheds some credible light on the entire debacle. What is also interesting is the article appeared in the early stages of the Great Recession.

Where Encompass Belonged

Roll-Up Aftermath

By Joe Salimando, Published September, 2003

Electrical Contractor Magazine

Just a few years ago, electrical construction consolidators sprang to life in a bizarre manner. Buying companies hand-over-fist and paying way too much, they added debt as if tomorrow would never come. But tomorrow is now here; for the most part, the consolidators are gone. What comes when dreams vanish and nightmares are revealed as 100 percent fluff?

Aftermath

In many cases, the "roll-up" trend wrought wholesale wreckage. As seen in the Wall Street bust, that is often the legacy of stock market-driven pursuits. Bankruptcy courts have been busy. Owners of equity or debt in these companies (even those still in business) have regrets.

Our aftermath includes — for some — new, more modest horizons. Ironically, many of these less grandiose "new" dreamers are the same people who sold out to the roll-ups in the first place. Back in electrical contracting, these executives (in many cases) run substantially the same companies they sold just a few years ago.

But the money men got around to the electrical niche. The prime example: Jonathan Ledecky of the Washington, D.C., area raised more than $500 million cash in what essentially was a "blind pool" in late 1997, via an initial public offering of stock.

Ledecky created Building One Services (BOSS was its stock symbol) and began buying electrical and mechanical contractors. Contractors were sold for a combination of cash and BOSS stock; tax advisors typically told sellers to take more in stock than cash (i.e., 45 percent cash, 55 percent stock).

With the company building effort not yet complete, Ledecky (and others) left the business, via a financial operation in which BOSS bought back their stock, taking on more debt. What was the result? Some fraction of the cash helped make Ledecky an owner of the Washington Capitals hockey team.

The meteors

Like a meteor, Encompass briefly lit up the skies. With more than $4 billion in annual sales in electrical/mechanical and janitorial contracting, it talked about providing building owners with one-stop "facility management services." This was similar to the strategy of EMCOR Group, which had been and still is the nation's largest electrical/mechanical contractor.

But meteors are described as shooting stars. Encompass became bankrupt in 2003. Why? Among other reasons, the company had an enormous amount of debt (some of it left over from that Ledecky buyout). Intangible assets (goodwill resulting from the many acquisitions) made its balance sheet asset light. The huge post-1999 reduction in data center and telecomm work also hurt Encompass.

Buddy and Paula Eidel were honored at the celebration.

Tri-City Electrical celebrates buy-back

On April 3, Altamonte Springs-based Tri-City Electrical Contractors Inc. hosted an event to celebrate its reacquisition by its management group headed by founder H.L. "Buddy" Eidel. Again privately owned and operated, Tri-City employs 1,200 workers statewide and operates divisional offices in Fort Myers, Jupiter, Ocala, Pompano Beach and Tampa. Tri-City has powered-up Florida for 45 years and has built its strong heritage on a business model philosophy to do more than is expected for the client, project and community.

Photos by Peter Barg

Southern Community Bank President Charles Brinkley, center, and Altamonte Springs Branch Vice President Tom Colletta, join in congratulating Buddy Eidel.

April 2003 Celebration of Tri-City buy back from Encompass

Electrical contracting companies acquired by Building One and Group Maintenance were sold off. Buyers typically included former owners or groups of managers — the folks who had sold out in 1998-2000.

Why were these buyers preferred? Most successful private electrical contracting companies are asset light. They own trucks, testing equipment and perhaps some lifts and, occasionally, the real estate on which the headquarters office stands. But a contracting company's value resides in its top people and work force — and the relation those humans create with customers.

Same as the old boss

Our aftermath, then, includes a significant number of large, independent, privately owned electrical contractors — similar companies to those operating in 1997, with similar or the same owners.

Integrity!

I first met Buddy Eidel at the Interlachen Country Club in 1985, when it was new. Since then, Buddy and I have played a lot of golf, socialized, and become good friends. Buddy is a great guy and he's not one to dominate a conversation. Instead, he contributes to it. You can't help but like him, and in fact I don't know of anyone who actually dislikes him. He's just a friendly, courteous, humble guy who did a great job building a major electrical contracting company.

In the early days, my wife, Carol, and I and Paula and Buddy, socialized at Interlachen. We'd have a drink or two and get dinner later on. Eventually, we invited one another to our homes or went out to eat. But, more than anything else, he and I talked business, mostly the similarities in the services we offered through our companies.

Although he was an electrical contractor, he'd developed an ongoing service and maintenance program for his clients. They provided a quality service, which was also a great way to ensure a recurring stream of revenues. We used Tri-City on all our homes and to this day, Tri-City takes care of all the serious electrical components.

Sometimes on Sundays, when the club holds a couples day, the four of us play a round of golf. The funny thing is, I can't recall a time when any of us got so frustrated with golf that someone threw a club ... particularly Buddy. He is as even-tempered as they get, and if his game was off, he just put his head down and kept working on his game.

As our country club continued to grow, a cadre of individuals emerged who wanted to make changes. Inevitably, a degree of discontent prompted the election committee to select Buddy as the club president. When he found out, he came to me and said, "If I'm going to do this, you've got to help me out." I said I would, so he appointed me Chair of the House Committee.

It wasn't long until a senior member suggested we replace the manager. Well, Buddy and I talked about it and agreed we should give everybody a fair shake. We talked with the manager and found him to be a pretty good guy with a great background. We also determined he was very capable, so Buddy and I agreed to work with him and give him our support. The Manager turned out to be a great asset to the Club.

To Buddy's credit, under his leadership the club made enormous progress. Members were happier, friendlier, and everything went along like clockwork. Buddy is not a campaigner nor crusader. He's just not that kind of guy, and people respect him for it.

I would trust Buddy Eidel with my last dollar. I know if Buddy told me he would do something, I could bank on the fact that he would do it. He is a man of integrity. He's a good family guy. He's a very intelligent man with a strong will and a strong character, and I love him like a brother. He and Paula have been our friends for a long, long time and that friendship has not changed to this day.

Harvey L. Massey - Massey Services, Inc.

8

Starting Over

At the time we bought the company back, we were fortunate to have some high accounts receivable in our books. When we reached out and collected on them over the next six months, we were able to pay back our short-term debt almost immediately. There were a few though, who

The Whole Family at Elbow Beach Marina, Bermuda - 2003

were reluctant to pay. They thought the bankruptcy situation meant they didn't have to take care of their obligations, so we took a few of them to court. We won of course. One of the debtors owed us $150,000, which was sorely needed, and a few others had to pay up as well through a court order.

We came out of the Encompass bankruptcy with around $35 million in backlog business. Once we got the bonding (with the help of our friend in Jacksonville), and once we had the financial situation under control with a line of credit, we were able to start building up the business again. We also paid the rest of our debts very quickly. Actually, it wasn't long until we were smoking right along, that is until around 2009 when the economy took a nose dive.

In 2008, we had revenue in the neighborhood of $190 million in current and backlog contracts. In 2009, we completed the Darden Restaurant Group Support Center with 1.14MW photovoltaic system, the largest private solar energy installation in Florida at the time. That all changed later in the year when the Great Recession really took hold. Then we had to go through the whole resizing thing again.

We probably waited a little too long and should have started earlier, but no one thought the downturn would last that long. As we all know by hindsight, most of the country found themselves in the same boat. We kept thinking we'd balance out, that the economy would rebound, until we finally had to make some tough decisions. Fortunately, we still had a couple of hefty contracts like Orlando's giant Amway Center, which we completed in late 2010.

The amazing part is, for quite some time we didn't lose any of our people. We wanted to sustain Buddy's legacy by keeping everyone employed regardless of how bad things were. Unfortunately, it didn't work out that way.

The first thing we did was freeze wages. Then we imposed a 10 percent across-the-board wage cut. We adjusted vacation time. Next, we took away paid holidays, including Memorial Day, Labor Day and the Friday after Thanksgiving. We also stopped contributing to the 401(k) program, and even had to take away personal days. There were adjustments to vacation days as well. We weren't very popular for all that, but we were in survival mode after all. Meanwhile, we kept beating the bushes to find new jobs. But there were scant opportunities out there: Everybody was in a slump. Everything around us had shrunk with the times.

9

Daybreak

We worked as close to the bone as possible through our already lean and mean organization. Even our fleet of service trucks kept going despite their high mileage. Case in point: my 2007 Tahoe had 343,000 miles on it before we considered replacing it. The takeaway? We had been changing out vehicles far earlier than necessary and our strict maintenance program had paid off. In fact, the recession taught us many things, and even when it was finally over we kept doing the same things to keep costs as low as possible.

A few people felt the austerity measures had left a bad taste in their mouth, but most of our employees understood. They wanted to help and were glad to have a job at all. They realized that even if they left, they'd have the same thing all over again somewhere else. We were so proud of everyone who stood tall with us as we took an economic pounding. Finally, the economy improved and things began to look better. Some of those who left during the Encompass days started to return. Eventually, we were able to reinstate benefits to where they were before the recession.

***

Not long ago, a few of us were gathered in a conference room on the fifteenth floor of an Orlando high rise. The owner of an out-of-town development company was there to plan the construction of a fairly tall building, so as a potential subcontractor we met with his team to

Today's Tri-City Executive Council - (L to R) CFO Mike Germana, President Jack Olmstead, Chairman Emeritus Buddy Eidel, Vice-President Rance Borderick

pitch our company. They weren't familiar with Tri-City, so the inevitable question about our track record came up: "I hear you've done quite a few jobs … that you've done this and you've done that. So, tell us what you've really built?"

Perfect timing, I thought. I asked the owner, the architect, and the engineer, to walk to the window with me. I gestured across the skyline and pointed to several prominent structures. "We built that, and that, and that, and that, and so on. I also pointed out the Amway Center and several other projects visible from that viewpoint. I told him about the George M. Steinbrenner Field in Tampa, the spring home of the New York Yankees, and the University of Central Florida's stadium, now known as Spectrum Stadium. Off to the right was the Dr. Phillips Center for the Performing Arts, and beyond sight but not far away was the Disney Springs project, completed in 2016. I told him we basically wired the entire city.

"You did all that?" he asked.

"Yeah," I said. "We've been around a while."

That window was probably the best testimony we could ever have.

Remembering Buddy and Tri-City by David Beasley

1

Rattling Walls

When I first laid eyes on Buddy Eidel, I saw a short man with black hair styled in flattop wearing thick, horned-rimmed glasses. He struck me as direct, hardworking, and honest … a man who did what he said he would do. That was in 1965, and he'd just hired me on as a journeyman electrician.

We got along very well and as time passed, I found we seldom did not see eye to eye. When we moved to the new building, our offices were adjacent to each other and I could sometimes hear Buddy and his dad talking. At times, they disagreed and the walls would actually rattle. Buddy could get on your case at times, and I remember being chewed out once in a while. One time when he brought in consultants, a couple of the guys made a few comments about them. Well, Buddy thought they were making fun of them, so he invited us to lunch where he chewed us out big time. I didn't have anything to do with it, but I got chewed out anyway.

I graduated high school in 1959 and immediately started in the electrical trade. I began by working for two contractors at Martin Marietta for a couple of years until they had a massive layoff. At the time, my dad, Barney Beasley, was superintendent with the construction firm that built the new McNamara Pontiac dealership. Tri-City did their electrical work, and it was their first big commercial contract.

Dad told me how great Tri-City was and recommended I talk with Buddy. I did, and Buddy hired me on. I was already a journeyman from Orlando, and back in those times you had to have licenses for every little city and municipality, so I had many licenses. When I joined Tri-City, there were less than twenty employees, and the company grossed around $700,000 per year. As a young electrician that sounded like a lot of money. But I didn't have much to compare that with in those days.

Three years later in 1968, Buddy asked me if I wanted to come in and do some estimating. I actually enjoyed working outside, but I talked it over with my wife that night and the next day I told Buddy I would come inside. Around that time, Fred Kroker also came inside to estimate and manage the residential division. Our offices were situated diagonally from Papa Eidel, and with Papa almost directly across from us with our doors open, he kind of kept an eye on all of us. He still had a thick German accent, was short in stature like Buddy, and of course his hair was all white and thinning on the top. And boy was he stringent! He'd often say, "We work hard and we play hard." Or, "When we work, we work. And when we play, we play." When I look back on those early days, I have only good memories.

2

Steak Dinner with Papa

I started out estimating apartments for the most part. At that time, an estimator's duties included buying the materials, arranging the work distribution, and managing the billing. In that sense, I was both estimator and project manager.

Buddy was always looking for ways to improve himself and the company. And he always put money back into the company for the facilities and employee educational programs. That was just a few of the effects I saw after he took that Harvard course, and I think that was one of the best things he did for himself.

While I was still an estimator, he invited a consultant named Paul Rodilla to help out. Paul said it would be a good idea to separate the company's purchasing, estimating, and project management divisions. After Paul left, Buddy asked if I wanted to continue as an estimator or a project manager. I said I'd like to be in management, so that's when I became the project manager for apartment and commercial work.

In 1980, Rance Borderick came into the office as an estimator and a project manager for housing and residential business. Later, in a meeting with Rance, Buddy, and a few others, I commented, "You know, the apartments used to be done with conduit, but later on they changed the code and the result was apartments are being done with Romex." That technical detail led to my next comment to Buddy: "Doesn't it make more sense to put the apartments under residential since both apartments and houses use Romex?" That's when both of those segments went over to Rance's jurisdiction. That's when I took over our commercial segment, our fleet, and our on-site storage units.

Around the time Buddy appointed me vice president and COO, I'd earned my private flying license. That came in handy because we'd opened our satellite offices and needed to get to them fairly frequently. I rented planes out of the Show Walter Airport — now the Orlando

Executive Airport — to fly Papa Eidel and others around to the branch offices. We'd examine the projects under way and walk through the sites to make sure they did what they should have. When the day was done, we flew back to Orlando and, after tucking the plane into its spot, usually stopped by a steak house where Papa bought dinner. It was a great way to wind the day down by talking about the projects and such. Papa was a real talker, and it was always fun to travel with him.

A few years later, I wound up buying my own airplane: a 1977 Cessna 182 four-seater that I rented back to Tri-City. The company owned a couple of Isuzu pickup trucks at the time, so I drove one to Fort Myers and one to Boynton Beach and left them near the airport. That way when I flew in we could drive a truck to the branch office instead of taking a taxi or bothering one of our employees. I also kept a 12-volt battery in the plane because sometimes the trucks sat a while and needed a jump-start.

In due time though, our workload in Orlando grew so big that I had to concentrate my time there. That was the end of our plane trips, so I sold the Cessna.

3

FEAT Begins

When Encompass got to the point they couldn't bid certain projects, it looked like they weren't going to survive. Then, when 2003 rolled around and things looked bad for the overall business, I left the company and joined Palmer Electric. My thought at the time was to make a deal with Palmer to become a large shareholder with them, thinking if we could build up Palmer we could hire some of the people from Tri-City after they went under. If it had stayed as it was with Buddy as the owner, I probably would not have left until I died.

Sometime in the early eighties, Buddy, along with Howard Palmer and Dan Petro —owner of Amber Electric in Orlando — decided there was a certain comingling of funds within ABC with their other programs. As a result, they pulled their money out and along with other interested companies developed the FEAT program. They did so in collaboration with Orange Technical College Mid Florida Campus in South Orlando. The purpose was to have a dedicated training program where donated funds were allocated for training and nothing else. There was no animosity with ABC, and they did an excellent job with the programs they had. Buddy and the others simply thought their training needs would be better met with a dedicated program for the construction trades.

With the help of ABC, we brought in representatives from the Orange County school system along with many other contractors, including plumbing, sprinkler contractors, carpentry, electrical, and other specialties into the mix. After many meetings and discussions, we started an in-school apprenticeship program called ACT: the Academy of Construction Technologies. Today, ACT is taught in the high schools by high school instructors who are paid by the county while the curriculum is developed by the industry. This gives students a jump-start on the trades so they can enter the FEAT program.

We also had special exemptions for students so they could work on the job site and their time and work would be applied toward credit for graduation. Buddy allowed me to take all the time needed to help the effort, and also gave considerable funding to get the program up and going.

We didn't have a training facility in some areas, so we established a working relationship with Seminole State College of Florida, where they taught the FEAT program. What followed were significant contributions to ACT by major contractors who started to plan, along with Seminole County officials, the construction of a building exclusively for the FEAT classes. About that time, I met with Daniel Webster, then Speaker of the Florida House of Representatives, and gave him our plans, write-up, and funding needs. It so happened we had friends in the construction industry, friends like State Senator Toni Jennings, the daughter of the owner of the Jennings Company. With their help and others in Tallahassee, we obtained state funding that was matched by industry participants. Now we could build the new training facility for both the ACT and FEAT students. As far as I know, Tri-City still supports that effort today.

My Take on the Beasley Family

Ever since David Beasley came to work for the company in 1965, the Beasley family has been synonymous with Tri-City Electric. In 1970, David's brother, Barney, worked for Tri-City's apartment house division followed by another brother, Donald Beasley. David's father, Barney Sr., was project manager during the construction of our new headquarters building. So, in a way, the Beasley clan became a bit of an institution in and around Tri-City, and every one of them worked hard.

Unfortunately, Barney Jr. passed away from skin cancer in the mid-eighties. A few years later his wife also passed away. David and his wife, Pat, took in their two daughters and raised them to adulthood.

I remember when David first went to work with us. One of his first jobs was the La Aloma Apartments on Semoran Boulevard for Earl Downs Construction Company. David worked with Bill Duym, another hard-working, long time Tri-City employee. Because of David and Bill's good work, we established strong, long lasting relationship with Earl Downs which opened the door to many more projects for his company.

David moved up through the ranks of the company and became my right-hand man for the production side of things. We decided he should manage all production in the Orlando area while I would be responsible for the branch offices. He went on to develop our detailed procedure manuals, many of which are still in use today.

I was saddened when David decided to leave the company in 2003, when it looked like Encompass would not survive. David was a valued and trusted employee and friend, and I was also sorry he had to leave his Tri-City career behind.

Buddy

Remembering Chuck McFarland by Buddy Eidel

After we experienced yet another growth spurt in the early nineties, I began to feel pressure from our main banker. He thought we should produce the quality of financial statements and information consistent with the size and type of company we'd become. I thought about that a while, and after due consideration decided to find a chief financial officer for Tri-City.

It took several months for me to pour over resume after resume, conducting several interviews with prospects, and eliminating all of them. When I came across Chuck's resume that found its way to me through a headhunter, I saw he had quite an impressive background with a large public electrical contractor. I called him in for an interview.

He struck me as a no-nonsense, hardnosed man with a soft, personable side. He was also a dedicated family man whose wife at the time was not in the best of health. He made it clear his main responsibility was to his wife and family, but that he would also be dedicated to his job. With priorities like that, I believed he was a good man as well as highly qualified for the job. After a few more interviews, I decided to hire him. On December 28, 1995, we made it official.

At the time, Chuck's daughter, Kelly, and son, Billy, were in school. In the afternoon during the week, Chuck picked them up from school and they did their homework on the conference table in his office until he was finished for the day. While that was unusual for a workplace, Chuck had already proven himself as a well-disciplined officer, so the arrangement never caused a problem. They were two lovely children, and we hardly knew they were there.

While I never regretted for one minute hiring Chuck, there were times we did not agree. Still, Chuck was a U.S. Navy man who always said he knew when to stand up, salute, and say "yes boss." He turned out to be a great sounding board for me for organizational and financial standpoints, yet he never tried to influence the production side of the business. He would always flag me when he saw a problem.

The bank definitely got what it asked for from Chuck because he redesigned our entire financial reporting system. He made the readouts clear and comprehensive for the banks as well as our managers, enabling them to use our job costing systems. Most of what he developed is still in use today. In addition to the banks, Chuck was also a great resource for our bonding relationships. He also reviewed all of our subcontract agreements with our general contractors, and worked on refining our purchasing systems in conjunction with my brother-in law, Robert Rudolph, who'd retired from the Jim Walter Corporation as their CFO.

What was unusual for a CFO numbers guy was that Chuck had an excellent sense of humor and we had many laughs and good times together. However, it should be said that it was not a good idea to get on his bad side, which is why I referred to him as my "New York junk yard dog." To that end, Chuck was a tremendous help when we structured the deal to sell the company to the New York investors. When everyone involved in the deal looked out for themselves, Chuck made sure he looked out for me.

It was a somewhat difficult time when we sold the company. I knew it was the right thing for my family and I, but I also wanted to look out for all our employees who'd spent so much of their lives helping me grow the business. Chuck helped me structure the deal in such a way that Building One Services would also provide stock to our main managers. I was convinced, maybe naively so, by Jonathan Ledecky when he said he did not want to make major changes in the company and intended to let us keep doing what we did best. However, during the time we were under Encompass, Chuck tried to advise the Encompass corporate leadership on some of the poor decisions they were about to make. But his advice mostly fell on deaf ears.

After the demise of Encompass, Chuck once again proved to be a valuable asset to the management team after the managers bought Tri-City from the bankruptcy court. Using his banking and bonding relationships, he helped rebuild the company financially. He also was a tremendous help navigating the company through the economic downturn that started in 2008.

Chuck passed away very suddenly on Dec 27, 2014, of a heart attack. It happened just short of his twentieth anniversary with the company. He was not only a very trusted and valuable employee, but a dear friend and mentor to me. We all miss him greatly.

A Positive Force

I'm proud to be part of a team that believes in our mission statement "Do more than expected." Tri-City cares about its' employees and shows it in countless ways. We are a family and are always there for each other, whether helping someone with an overload of work or making a casserole for someone in a family crisis. It's the best job I've ever

---

had, and it's a great feeling to look forward to going to work each day.

Buddy Eidel always said, "You work *with* me, not for me." One day I asked him how he accomplished everything in front of him each day, and his answer taught me an important life lesson. He said, "You need to organize your work so you are tackling the most difficult tasks early on while you're fresh, and save the easier work for later in the afternoon." I've incorporated that and it works wonderfully, both on a professional and personal level.

Regardless of his heavy schedule, Buddy had an open door policy and always made time for the employees regardless of rank. He is a humble man who never forgot how he and Papa started out by knocking on doors looking for work. This year, Tri-City will celebrate sixty successful years, but instead of patting himself on the back and taking credit for his success, he gives all the credit to his employees.

I also have the pleasure of knowing Paula Eidel, and she and Buddy are the perfect match. They work together, have fun together, and have love and respect each other.

Many years ago, Tri-City had to decide on a new phone system: at the time voice mail and automated answering messages were getting big. Buddy and I discussed the positives of voice mail, but thank goodness he made it clear that there would always be a live voice answering the phone. Thank you for making that decision, Buddy!

> I am truly blessed to have Buddy Eidel as a part of my life. He has been such a positive force to me, and I look forward to his continued sunshine in my life when he comes to Tri-City for monthly meetings.
>
> **Elizabeth (Liz) Marshe – Receptionist/ Administrative Assistant Since 1988**

What's Next for Tri-City? by Jack Olmstead

Although Buddy *officially* retired at the end of 2000, it seems as if it was just a few years ago. Buddy continues as our Chairman Emeritus and always looks forward to joining us at our annual board meeting, as well as our monthly financial meetings and various employee functions. We so appreciate and enjoy the wisdom and input he brings; he always has something of value to add, as well as throwing out an occasional "Buddy-ism."

In the past fifteen years, Tri-City has travelled a long and sometimes very challenging road. We have had our share of ups and downs with the economy, and have always maintained an attitude that we would make it through the tough times. And, when we could, we built up for the future tough times. That is what all good business people should do, and that is exactly what Buddy did.

February 27, 2017 marked our fourteenth anniversary of acquiring the company and returning it to a private entity. That was the year we formed an ESOP, an Employee Stock Ownership Plan. We looked at many formulas for the company's future success, but in perpetuity, the ESOP was the ultimate program that made the most sense for both ownership and employees. It offers employees an additional vehicle for retirement planning, and enables us to keep the family culture and values established by Buddy sixty years ago.

At this time, business is great and there is an abundance of work but as history has taught us, our industry is cyclical. Based on past experience, we continue to operate lean and mean so that we are positioned securely no matter how the economy may swerve. We also pay close attention to our vertical markets, to make sure we have trained personnel experienced in whatever industry is growing. For example, we were prepared for the huge upswing in national health care; in fact, we have a dedicated health care team that is well versed on the special needs for that particular market. Our "ride and show" teams working in the entertainment and theme parks of Central Florida have grown due to the huge expansions taking place at this time. The ability to compete and build effectively in the multi-family sector has provided a major advantage for our company throughout Florida.

We are on a constant lookout for better technology and best practices of installation. With advances in technology such as LED lighting and sophisticated control systems for the consumption of electricity, our industry will always be around. Keeping abreast of all these changes is necessary to stay ahead, which is why a young person starting out in a company like Tri-City will find unlimited opportunities to grow.

We are utilizing the most up-to-date software for project management for nearly all of our jobs. It starts in estimating, continues to the project manager, and goes all the way to the completion of the project. Again, this technology keeps us ahead of most of our competition in efficiency and profitability.

We share our best practices and gain knowledge developed at other companies through our participation in the Peer Group, where we candidly discuss how we can better ourselves. When multiple companies work together in a noncompetitive manner like the Peer Group, highly productive, innovative practices result. These are put in place immediately since they have already been established by one or more Peer Group members.

We have enhanced our pre-fabrication shop with the latest and greatest tools that cuts our production time, allowing us to utilize less manpower at the site and to control material waste. This is a great place to bring new people into our company and let them learn from ground up in the shop. Later, they can transfer to a project with knowledge of material, and experience building assemblies.

We are always searching for quality employees, and that's where we have an advantage: good people want to work with the good people at Tri-City, which has the best in the business all the way from field personnel to management. We take advantage of, or create if necessary, training opportunities and then we reward initiative.

We wholeheartedly support unique programs such as Workforce Development. We also work closely with ABC to educate our representatives in Tallahassee as well as Washington as to the importance of trade education initiatives. We sponsor events like the annual Build Tampa Bay, where we introduce high school students to our varied and lucrative career paths. We actually have a signing ceremony similar to the NFL draft, where graduates put on a hard hat and commit to joining a construction company.

As Buddy often did, I also like to visit, or "stomp around some jobs." By doing so, I can keep an ear to the ground regarding our safety practices and stay closer to our crews and field leadership as to potential improvements.

Of course, there is much more going on that I haven't mentioned. Suffice it to say, because we have such a great team of workers, Tri-City Electrical Contractors will continue to go from success to success.

IV
THE YEARS SINCE RETIREMENT

1

An Unwanted Visitor

One would think that after all the years of building a family and a business, that the relative inactivity of retirement would bring peace and renewed health. Well, that was not the case with me, so what I'm about to relate will hopefully serve as a warning.

On March 12, 2014, my seventy-fifth birthday, I went for my semi-annual physical with our primary care doctor, Ivan Castro. The results of my previous examination were all negative, meaning everything was fine. But this time the doctor found a lump on the left side of my neck. I'd never noticed it before, but he said it was either a swollen lymph node or a lymphoma, and that we'd have to wait a month to see if it went away. Needless to say, when I heard "lymphoma" my heart jumped to my throat. Everyone dreads that "C" word.

When I returned to Dr. Castro the following month, the lump was still there and my journey through treatment, and eventual cure, began. Dr. Castro immediately sent me to Dr. Jeffrey Baylor of Ear, Nose, Throat, & Plastic Surgery Associates in Orlando. Dr. Baylor confirmed I had two squamous cell tumors far back in my throat, only visible by running a scope through my nose and on down. Worse yet, he said the lymph nodes on my neck were probably malignant.

My next appointment was with Dr. Henry Ho, an Otolaryngology surgeon. Dr. Ho performed surgery on May 20 of that year and removed the two squamous cell tumors as well as a pocket of lymph nodes in my neck, which also turned out to be malignant. Dr. Ho said the surgery was successful and he had removed all the cancer. After surgery, it was decided I should undergo both chemotherapy and radiation.

Dr. Ho sent me to Dr. Lee Zenhgebot of Hematology & Oncology Consultants, who prescribed a series of chemo treatments. Then I saw Dr. David Diamond of Florida Radiation and Oncology Group who prescribed my radiation treatments. Both doctors suggested I have a feeding tube inserted into my stomach, since both treatments would prevent me from swallowing. Paula was devastated by the idea of a feeding tube and thought the treatment would kill me rather than cure me. But all the doctors — including a second opinion — assured us it was the right way to go and that I would be cured. We both knew it would be difficult, but agreed we would remain positive, and "up" for the challenge.

The chemo and radiation treatments ran concurrently from the end of June through the end of August of that year. They made me very weak, and I even lost my voice for a few weeks, which was extremely scary. Nevertheless, through the help and support of my wife, family, and friends, I made it through. When I reflect on all that occurred in those months, I truly believe the treatment of the patient by the caregiver is as hard, if not harder, on the caregiver than on the patient. But Paula was my rock throughout the whole ordeal.

Like any crisis, close, caring friends and family will draw near to give support, so I'd like to acknowledge a few of them. One special friend, James Campbell, experienced the same kind of throat cancer and went through a similar treatment. James was a tremendous support and gave me good insight about what to expect. He often told me there definitely is a light at the end of the tunnel. I will always be indebted to James for his support.

Our very good friends, Ed and Susan White were also very supportive. Ed and Susan go to the same church we do, All Saints Episcopal Church in Winter Park, and they encouraged Paula and me to attend a healing service there. When an evil thing like cancer creeps into a body rendering a person almost defenseless, divine healing is also welcome. So, we went, and whether my healing came directly from above or through the hands of His physicians, the healing took place.

My dentists, Drs. Thomas and Abufaris, were both extremely helpful and supportive of my treatment. I am indebted to Dr. Castro who found the original lump and raised the alarm. I feel like he saved my life with the early detection of the tumor.

The experience gave me a renewed sense of faith. Many prayers went up on my behalf, for which I am eternally grateful. If I did not realize it before the cancer, I realized afterwards how much I was loved by my wife, all my children, and my friends. As of this writing, I am doing very well, and my periodic checkups with the doctors confirm there is no new activity.

As a final word, my warning to you is this: be sure to get regular checkups!

***

In addition to my life, faith, and appreciation, my attitude in respect to where we lived changed as well. I realized that if I got sick and could no longer maintain our home, we should consider other living arrangements. We had a beautiful, ten-year-old home on Lake Osceola in Winter Park. While living on a lake was wonderful, the house was quite large and brought a very high maintenance schedule with it. So, we started to look around at condominiums in our area.

In July of 2017, we found an ideal place at The Residences condominiums in downtown Winter Park. It is a corner unit on the fifth floor with windows on three sides, and all on one floor. We'll have 24/7 concierge service, and an elevator opens to our foyer. We closed the sale in September of 2017, and as of this writing are just about finished with the extensive remodeling project. And with perfect timing, we closed on the sale of our Greentree Drive lake house in February of 2018.

Don't Look in the Living Room!

I first met the Eidels many years ago when Paula called our company, Ewing Noble & Winn Interiors, about redecorating their family room on Alabama Drive. I remember walking in to have a look, and on the way I glanced into their living room. When she saw me checking it out she said, "That is not the room we want to do over; no one ever goes in there." I replied, "Hmmm, I'm not surprised. They thought my comment was hilarious.

The family room was not such a big deal really. Paula insisted we include a comfy easy chair for Buddy, and on the evening of our install I called to see if Buddy liked his chair. He replied, "Tell Sam to do the entire house over." Typically, in our business, the husband's role is to keep the reigns on the checkbook, but that wasn't Buddy's style at all. He played an entirely different part, and on many occasions he was the one who was fairly loose with the checkbook. He'd say, "Come on Paula, let the experts do this."

For every meeting, Buddy arrived with a complete agenda printed out on a spreadsheet detailing what we'd do that day. Then after the day's work, my team was emailed the "minutes" of what took place that day, neatly printed out, with footnotes, just like a boardroom. In my forty-five years of doing this business, I have never experienced that kind of close interaction.

Buddy was incredibly detail-oriented and thoroughly organized, which I suppose is the reason he grew such a successful business. Working with them is one of the best experiences in all the years I've been designing homes.

During our first project with the Eidels — the house on Alabama Drive — one of Paula's concerns was that we asked her to pick out furniture from pictures rather than actually sitting on the upholstery. I assured her that my business partner, Gail Winn, and I only provided our clients with the most comfortable furniture. Both Buddy and Paula were pleased with our selections.

Sometime later, they built their summer house in New Smyrna Beach and we were involved again. Our in-house architect did the design and of course, Buddy kept us organized all the way. That house turned out spectacularly. During that time, I'd planned to build a 5,000-square-foot "spec" house on a lake in Winter Park. We just knew Buddy would like the plans, so I told him all about the project.

After finishing the project and on our drive back to the office, I told Gail that our spec house would be perfect for the Eidels. Literally minutes later, my phone rang. It was Paula. She said they were interested the lake house and wanted to look at the lot and plans. Well, they bought it. So, we were off on another adventure. Just recently they decided to downsize, so they sold their home on the lake and bought a condo in Winter Park. One more time, Gail and I had the pleasure of working with them.

One of the side benefits of working with them was that Gail, her husband, Mike, Paula, Buddy, and I became great friends. It is so great when nice things happen to deserving people, and Buddy and Paula are certainly deserving people. We always enjoyed our time together and they always made it fun.

Buddy and Paula are folks with incredible integrity, which is the highest compliment I can give. They are as good as it gets.

Sam Ewing

2

Foundations

When I originally started my business, I only wanted to make money and work for myself rather than for someone else. I also wanted a way to provide for my family. As the business matured, I discovered I really wanted to be a successful contractor in Florida's growing construction industry. It wasn't long until I found out how much I didn't know.

My bankers and bonding companies always pushed and pressured my company to do better. Fortunately, due to my Harvard experience, I realized I needed to surround myself with capable management people, good business systems, and experienced electricians.

When something didn't work with a manager, I had a difficult time changing course. So, Paula and I often put our heads together to arrive at the right tactic. She didn't want a bad situation to linger and get worse. The first thing Paula would say when something wasn't right was, "What are we going to do about it?" If a job wasn't going well, we tried to find

CHARLIE CRIST
GOVERNOR

September 19, 2008

Dear Friends:

Congratulations to Tri-City Electrical Contractors on celebrating your 50th anniversary!

As you celebrate this milestone in the history of Tri-City Electrical Contractors, spend time reflecting on the many accomplishments that have led to the company's success. Tri-City Electrical Contractors has played a vital role in the community by providing quality services to citizens. Recognized by *Southeast Construction Magazine* as the fifth largest specialty contractor in the Southeast and the 25th largest electrical contractor in the United States, Tri-City is a role model for many companies throughout the Sunshine State.

Thank you to Tri-City Electrical Contractors for your commitment to serve citizens in your community. Your dedication has impacted the lives of countless individuals.

Congratulations on celebrating your 50th anniversary!

Sincerely,

Charlie Crist

THE CAPITOL
TALLAHASSEE, FLORIDA 32399 • (850) 488-2272 • FAX (850) 922-4292

Our 40th in Paris

Our 40th Atop the Eiffel Tower

the reason why and then fix it. Then we tried to learn from that and not do the same thing in the future. That always spurred me on to figure out a new approach.

I remember the old saying, "A person needs to run his business with his head, not his heart." I believed that was partly true, so my approach was a compromise with that philosophy. I'd seen too many heartless businesses that were not morally successful, and to me success in business meant *both* financially and morally. In that vein, I'm grateful to my mother and father for teaching me how to work hard and be responsible at the same time. It is important to be able to look at oneself in the mirror and know you are right with the world.

Today, Tri City continues to be a tremendous company. I will take credit for establishing the foundation, culture, and systems we put in place, including hiring good people who believed in that culture and foundation. Jack Olmstead, Rance Borderick, CFO Mike Germana, and our management team all have continued our success. Never in my dreams did I think our company would reach the heights that the current team has achieved. It has not always been easy, and as surely as tides rise and fall, good and bad times will come again. But, Jack, Rance, Mike, and all our fine employees have demonstrated their ability to navigate through the tough times back into the good ones. Tri-City will persevere.

3

An Homage to Others Like Us

What amazes me is the number of successful Central Florida general contractors that started a few generations ago and remain to this day. They began with a grandfather, and then their son or daughter took over, followed by a grandson, granddaughter, or other family members. I had the pleasure of knowing many of those patriarchs as well as their offspring, on down to today. I'll point out a few.

There is the Jennings family of Jack Jennings & Sons Construction Services . Jack, the father, started the business and today is led by his daughter, Toni, and sons Jeff and John. The Kelsey family of Eugene Kelsey Construction Company started in 1920 with grandfather and founder Eugene Kelsey. Gene Kelsey, Eugene's son, had the reins it until his sons, Mike and Bob Kelsey, took over. The fourth generation has Mike Kelsey's daughters, Courtney K. Peacock and Monica J. Lockwood with the company. The H. J. High Construction Company of Orlando, was founded by Steve Highs father, Johnny High. Johnny passed away just after I started in business. Steve High's son Robert took over the business and is currently president of the business. It is marvelous to see that kind of legacy passed on from generation to generation.

Here are a few more:

- The Williams Company Orlando Florida, founded by brothers Randell & Ralph Williams, and then cousins Bruce and Alan Williams.
- Walker Construction Company of Winter Park, Florida. Lance Walker, Sr. is President and Joe Fisher is Vice President. R. Lance Walker, Jr, Lance's son, is now Vice President. Lance and Joe started business in 1974.
- W.A. McCree Construction began in 1926 with W.A. McCree Sr. His son, Bert McCree, was next in line to manage business, and then his son, Richard McCree, Sr., followed by Richard McCree Jr., who is currently with the company.

I am grateful to have known these good men and women throughout my career. The fact that they were there working alongside Tri-City Electrical Contractors was always a source of inspiration for me. There are many, many more like these and I'm sure they had a major impact on their sphere of business as well. I consider the above and others out there, part of our unique business community.

Looking Back

As the saying goes, "Behind every successful man, stands a strong, loving woman." Paula is truly a prime example of that. She has been my rock in making both family and business decisions. She has nursed me through ill health as well as been my playmate. We've snow skied together, golfed together, travelled the world together, and celebrated every holiday and family birthday together. When I was running the company, she handled all our personal finances to the point where I'd ask, "Do we have any money, and if so can I have some for my wallet?"

I count on her to make me look good in every respect, and in response, she will say that I make *her* look good. Like my Harvard dorm roommate, Sam Kind, said, "When you hit the ball and it lands right in the middle of the fairway in a perfect spot, it doesn't get any better than that!" Well, that describes our marriage.

Paula will say we are best friends. She will say she loves my company, and that I am her hero, and she'll say we know how to have fun. Because of her, we have many friends. Some people think she is the brains behind the outfit, but she will say I'm the smart one and she only enhances what I do. We both know how to work hard and play hard.

Together, we raised five wonderful children and seven grandchildren. We adore our family and could not be prouder of them. We have lived a fabulous life, and for that, we are filled with gratitude. Lucky us. We found the brass ring!

Eidel Legacy at Christmas 2008 at Greentree Drive home

Daughter Joyce and Husband, Harvey Rose at TCE 50th Anniversary –
2008

Daughter Bethany, Husband, John Canfield, and their son, Jackson at TCE's 50th – 2008

Daughter Tammy and husband, Reed Collins at TCE's 50th – 2008

John Canfield and son Jackson Canfield at 5oth anniversary party

Paula & Buddy at 50th TCE anniversary – 2008

The Goldey Family (L to R): Dylan, Madeline, Stacia, & Clark at Tri-City's 50th Anniversary

Son Scott Haffner - 2017

Made in the USA
Columbia, SC
31 October 2018